ETCHINGS

fiction
essays
photography
poetry
art

ETCHINGS

2

Edited by
Sabina Hopfer
Christopher Lappas
Patrick Allington

Published by ILURA PRESS
Melbourne Australia

ETCHINGS

ILURA PRESS
PO Box 680
Elsternwick VIC 3185
Ph/Fax: +61 3 9533 0794
Email: etchings@ilurapress.com
Web: www.ilurapress.com

Published by Ilura Press

Etchings 2, 2007
ISBN 978 1 921325 00 7
ISSN 1833-9654

DESIGN AND LAYOUT: Ilura Press

COVER ART: Basil Eliades
Detail from ***The River of Her Immense Stupidity***, 2002

Printed and bound by BPA Print Group, Burwood, Victoria

Subscriptions & Submissions

Subscription Rates
3 issues (1 year)

	Individual	**Institution**
Australia	AU$68	AU$98
New Zealand	AU$72	AU$104
Asia/Pacific	AU$78	AU$112
USA/Canada/Middle East	AU$84	AU$122
Europe/Rest of the World	AU$89	AU$128

For full subscription details, please refer to the *Etchings* website:
www.ilurapress.com/Etchings.html

Submissions

Postal submissions:
Send submissions as A4, hard-copy, double-spaced to *Etchings*, Ilura Press, PO Box 680, Elsternwick VIC 3185, Australia.

Electronic submissions:
We also accept electronic submissions, particularly from overseas contributors. Email submissions to etchings@ilurapress.com

Please limit submissions to three stories, three poems, or three images.

Also include a cover letter and a short bio with your submission.

For full information and guidelines, please refer to the *Etchings* website:
www.ilurapress.com/Etchings.html

Contents

Poetry

Essays

Art/Photography

EDITORIAL

After a successful debut, *Etchings* is once again filled with a cosmopolitan mix of writing, remaining true to its mission to juxtapose Australian writing with writing from around the world, and to adopt an international approach by exchanging and communicating ideas across borders.

With the Internet becoming one of the most powerful mediums to date for travelling across cultures, the push and pull, the intermingling, of local and global ideas has become an everyday reality.

In this issue, John Tranter, acclaimed poet and founding editor of the online magazine *Jacket*, as well as speaking about his own poetry, takes us into cyberspace where literature and stories are collected and distributed without boundaries. *Jacket* has become one of the world's most widely read poetry magazines. By opening up poetry to the Web, Tranter has managed to establish a global portal for poets, creating an audience that is by far larger than it could ever be in any specific geographical place at any one time.

As much as there exists a buzz over the potential of the Internet, there is always the potent energy that is created by artists themselves. We find that precise exuberance in the work of Melbourne poet, sculptor, and painter Basil Eliades. Particularly his paintings exude an encapsulating, all-embracing energy, reflecting a desire to penetrate, transcend, and connect with the Australian landscape.

Narratives generate energy, and narratives come in many forms. History creates one form of narrative, and fiction another. In the context of Australian literature, Dominique Hecq in her essay 'Passports to the Past' ventures into the controversial domain of historical versus fictional truth. She explores the experience of exile and the ruptured notion of history that comes with it, claiming that fiction creates a connection between the past and the present as valuable and vital as the one assigned to history.

Translators are responsible for another form of connection, namely that between original text and translated text, between original language and target language, between one culture and another. Ton That Quynh Du explores the (in)visibility of the translator, talking about his experience of translating the work of the Vietnamese writer Pham Thi Hoai into English.

And last but by no means least, our fiction and poetry, once again the connective tissue of *Etchings*, take the reader into the streets of Sydney, New York, Edinburgh, into a Thai village, a retirement home, a candlelit room where tradition, philosophising, and a modern marriage in Vietnam collide, over jazz-filled rooftops, and deep into the darker recesses of the mind.

SABINA HOPFER

God's Holding Paddock

Jane Downing

It all started ... well it probably all started a long time back, but I haven't got all day. Though that is just a catch-phrase and of course I have. All day, every day.

They say talking to yourself like this is the first sign of madness. A sign, one of many on the great journey of life. But we're not out cruising on the highway anymore, one sign sprouting alone up ahead, barely discernable in the distance. There's a veritable forest of signs here now, thick and undeniable, as we lurch into city central, heading toward the Great Terminus where I will not, *will not*, let myself end up a bag lady, rummaging in the bins with brooding fingers and rheumy eyes.

So I couldn't remember the name of the spoon I was holding. I stood at the sink letting sunbeams dance off its curves, shivers of migraine against the eyes. Thinking: the owl and the pussycat. I was all at sea with the beasts until I latched onto *runcible* spoon. But the triumph died. I've never owned a runcible spoon, and who but the owl and the pussycat, for their slices of quince, ever did? I put what happened to be a dessert spoon in the drawer and hoped I'd be able to pick the right word up later.

It's awful when all those words on the tip of the tongue move further and further back. You can gag on them; or just feel horribly queasy. One day I won't even notice they're completely gone. I left the rest of the breakfast dishes (hardly worthy of the plural) to dry on the draining board and went and sat on the old kitchen chair by the back door. Cracked vinyl and liver-spotted metal legs are overlooked, as I hope others will overlook my own growing decrepitude. The seat serves for when my legs find the journey from the garage to the back door onerous. It waits by the outside tap, in company with the bucket and mop which I must put away, and I remember its prime, when it was one of a set of four, new and proudly carried into the kitchen by Bob one hot Saturday afternoon.

That's not the point, though. Old people can spend too much time looking back. Or digging amongst the eroding roots for buried bones. Acting like they're in the epilogue of their lives, all the action and adventure gone before. Gone. But it is not so: there is a future. I have to look at it now, while I still can. There's only one kitchen chair left, and not much time. I sat on the vinyl to purposefully rid my mind of spoons.

Camellias, azalias, roses, I recited, moving my eyes around the garden. Easy enough to remember: they were always there. I still potter about when my knees allow me to kneel—there are annuals to prove it. Ranunculus, stocks, sweet pea, sweet William, violets, viola, verbena, petunia, zinia (soon), nusturtium (by the compost), and not to forget, forget-me-nots. See? My relieved sigh was genuine. I'd met the challenge. All the words tumbled out without a hiccup, without a pause, tripping over the tip of my tongue. I still had it in me: my memory, that is. Surely I could stop my obsessive collecting of stories, old people stories, real ones, not from books or novels, arranged in an album in my mind like stamps, or on a shelf like shells, or pinned like moths. Stories to measure myself against. The hints and clues to what I should do next.

Should I hang about like Mrs Patterson opposite who waited till it was too late and died in front on the television? No knowing who saw her off: Ray Martin or Don Burke, or those nice police from Sun Hill. Her children appeared from nowhere to clean up the house, plonking a large blue Cleanaway hopper on the curb like an oversized tombstone. At the end of the day old Mrs Patterson's handbag was sitting on the peak of a mountain of rubbish that had been her life. Perched on top. As, in life, it had perched on her lap. She never left the house without it. Too sad. Too much. So should I move out while there is still time like the couple on the corner? Though *she* should have waited, of course. The proportion of women to men in those places is forbidding. At least one will be wanting to steal her Cyril. Some of these tarts had to be the ones taking up with American GIs in the War. Age does not weary ... it never stops.

But apparently Mr Wintergarten is happy as Larry in the better place he shuffled off to. *Have to move. I could cook for myself, only Edna spoilt me*, he told me at his wife's funeral. He breakfasts with six ladies in their best cardigans and pearls. So his daughter said when I ran into her at the 7-Eleven. Putting a spin on it probably. He'd have to polish his pate and put his teeth in every morning. The pros and cons. Yes, the pros and cons see-sawed as I sat, as they have for donkey's ages. To go or to stay? Eighty is just around the corner. And it's impossible to see around corners.

I don't want to leave it until it's too late: when paranoia has set in and there's a man lurking behind every camellia, when the family next door raise their eyes to heaven and exchange in whispers, *she's not herself.* What is it to be yourself? I won't know then. I won't know to put a brave face on it.

I composed it, my face, there on the chair, the Nile delta around each eye, great tributaries down the cheeks. God is kind, and as the looks fade so does the eyesight. I can imagine myself serene. Or merry and lively, eyes dancing to pick up the next stray story.

The garden was looking a picture that morning. I know the colours are going, not blanching in the unforgiving sun, but fading through the filter of my milky cataracts, which is where precious memory serves. Beautiful like a painting, my garden, I told myself. We could pretend it was like Monet's Givinchy paintings, he who had his own trouble with cataracts. We needn't admit it is more like one of Picasso's later paintings.

There was a noise in the kitchen behind me. A click, a shuffle.

'Bob?' I'd share the joke with him. 'Put the kettle on while you're there. I'd love a cup.'

There was no reply.

I didn't cry. I don't anymore. No point if there's no comforting hand to reach across, no sympathetic eyes. Which there haven't been since Bob died three years ago. Well, two years and nine months, it just seems longer.

See, I had to do something before it was too late.

Most days my only communication, except with myself, is with the magpies. They bring their chicks back each year and strut up the garden path as if they own the place. What will they do if the new owner appears at the back door not with crackers and bits of bacon rind, but with a rush away to work and life outside this little domestic sphere? How many years will they swoop back with junior, two black cloaks of complacency with a demanding grey shadow? They are the image of me and Bob in the early days, with Greg one step behind, Greg who lives in London now and cannot be burdened because his kids, the younger generation, still pull and squawk.

I practiced my pitch on the magpies until I sounded composed, rational and just the type of old lady the Home would want. They mustn't suspect me for the barmy old bat I am. My story collection helped me in my choice of who to ring. I shuffled through the stories, retrieving names from the file in my cerebellum. Retirement Villages, Nursing Homes and everything in between. Some must be okay. I needn't go imagining they'd all be as dire as in those miserable novels, though some were, of course. The Salvo place wouldn't get a call. I'd heard residents there were legless—in both or either sense. Old age does not automatically make good citizens of us. 'Old and wise' is just another catch-phrase. How would I go living with a lot of old people? I almost didn't make the call, again.

I wasn't having anything to do with anything that had Twilight in the name. Were we riding off into the sunset like great heroes? Only the black of night comes after the twilight. On the other hand, The Haven seemed the obvious choice, not only for the obvious meaning. It's also one letter from Heaven. If the owners were into wordplay, it augured well. I considered that I could be deluded as well as demented, but the woman on the line seemed kind. Kind without calling me dear. Essential qualities not nearly lauded enough.

First impressions and all, I was careful with my face that morning. Not too much makeup, you know those old ladies who look like something out of a vaudeville show. Mutton dressed up as ham. I steadied the lipstick, minimising the creep into the canyons of wrinkles round the mouth with a hanky, which I tucked into the top of my bra for emergencies. My underclothes were also clean. Hanky, clean underwear, what was the third thing we had to tell Greg when he left the house? Those essentials should an Ambulance-man have to pick you up after an accident. She said them all the time, too. She? I mustn't say she. I was told always to use names. She is, after all, the cat's mother. Which she also admonished all the time: that is, the she who was my mother. Hanky, clean underwear, I rummaged in my bag—keys? No that wasn't it. Mother never drove. She—my mother, not the cat's—turned her toes up at home. No nursing home interventions on her heart, lungs, circulation, cataracts, to keep her going. Like a pet, she was alive, and then she was dead. We could have just buried her under the jacaranda. But how can I do as she did? It would be inconsiderate to Greg, who is probably somewhere in London without a clean hanky, or underwear—the British are *notorious*.

Without the third safeguard for emergencies, whatever it is, I had to leave the house. It took most of the morning: just getting out. I was slowing down fast, even as I watched myself. I felt like I had my arm out the window, like in our first car, fluttering my hand up and down to indicate this slowing down. But was my hand visible to everyone else? Or, like the men in the 1950s scoffed, did it simply look like I had my hand out drying my nail polish? Now, of course, we have break lights on the back of the car. When I stop completely, will they come on? Seems more appropriate that they go off. I'm sure I'll forget to raise my hand, out of the driver's window in a Red Indian *How*. Stop, it meant in the old days before lights. But, how, how, how did I get here? I was going to my car. It took most of the morning.

My little 1966 Torana was already getting hot inside. It'd have to be sold. *Only one old lady driver,* the ad would read. *Using it for Bingo on Fridays.* A teenager would buy it and paint flowers down the side, or overstuff the ashtray with butts.

Ye gods and little fishes, I told myself at this point, as I often have to. The Torana's future was not my worry. My future loomed. Turn right at *The Star*, the kind lady on the phone had said. The pub casts shadow lace on the pavement. Shadows of its wrought iron self. Myself. A shadow. Once iron. Still wrought. Or overwrought to be more accurate.

I'd thought it was strange, using a pub as a landmark to direct sober old women, but the opposite corner alerted me to the diplomacy in it. The funeral parlour was big and new. Business was obviously booming. The Haven was but a holding paddock for this next move. Death. See, I can say it, yet even I hadn't known it could be quite so final until it took Bob. Bob would know what I should do. He was good at making decisions. When he went—via a parlour smaller, older—only the pain let me know I was still alive. He'd been a lousy driver, though. Always too fast, too impatient. He'd be moaning all the way along this road. *Well, where is it then?* Accelerating, braking abruptly at any large gates, speeding just when the exasperation of the driver behind was about to give.

The Haven was a long way out. I was driving and driving to the very sky's end. Where God will find you, even should you go so far. They say. There were no impressively large gates to announce The Haven's entrance; when it finally came I had to do a U-turn to double back and that man had no right to tootle so vigorously. Couldn't he see my hand out the window to show I was turning? No gates, only a sentinel row of agapanthus, in bloom. But I found it.

First impressions? What would they think of me, but also what did I think of it? This was no rambling estate like in the movies. There'd be no peacocks mournfully crying at apposite moments in the day. Nothing highfalutin at all. Though goodness knows what falutin is; probably wouldn't want any of the stuff, low or high. The reception building is ordinary, a rather unfortunate blonde brick which really should be banned. Still, it's not such a bad thing to look unpromising—expectations can only be bettered.

I was met by a kindly guide and taken first to the independent units, which would be my first step also, should I decide to come. The Haven is an entire village, care graded until The End (which is never directly mentioned in the brochure). I was introduced to an old lady, who may even be my age. Genetics, environment, nutrition, exposure to sunlight—our days in the sun—obscure, confound and confuse the passing of time. Not quite Einstein's theory of relativity, which I could see I would not be discussing here.

The old lady took my hands, patting them. Reassuring. Or in need of reassurance? 'I lost my license, you see,' she smiled. 'They are kind here. And what would I do without a car otherwise?' Her hands were so soft. Mine are gnarled and callused, used to the soil and the spade, when my knees allow it. Hers were as soft as ... as tissues, as a pillow? As cool as an autumn creek? No, nothing quite describes them. Next time I feel something this soft and cool though, I'll know it's as soft as an old woman's hands.

'I have my own kitchen, and I can go to The Haven on Wednesdays for Selena to wash and set my hair.' The hands patted the heartening news into mine. She had hair like an angel's halo floating above her crab-apple face.

I turned from the human mirror. Time here was short as I was to join morning tea within the nursing home itself. To meet *the crowd*, my guide called them. Like teenagers hanging around with their crowd, so must we.

With crowds you don't at first notice individual faces. Just as you don't pick one voice from a chorus, one instrument from an orchestra. All combine to make an impression. Harmony or discord. I tried to hum in harmony with my brain as I entered the sea of decrepitude, the ocean of frailty. The little billabongs of feebleness off to the side. I didn't want to look into the individual faces. God had forgotten them. Why hadn't He come to take them here at the sky's end?

'We celebrate special occasions,' said my guide to this underworld portal. 'It is Mavis Balbilini's 100th birthday.' Mavis was the one propped in front of a hundred candles. Blowing would extinguish all breath from her mastectomied chest. Her eyes twinkled, though. Or was it only the reflection of the flames? No, her mouth smiled too.

'Reminds me of an Odd Spot in *The Age*,' said a voice at my elbow. He was in his pyjamas, and offering me the chair beside his. His false teeth sat on his lap, to better suck dunked arrowroots with his naked gums. Nursing home romances? Unimaginable. Impossible. That'd be more than an Odd Spot in *The Age*.

'Silly season story,' he continued without hearing my polite thanks for the seat. Either he was deaf or had perfected the male skill of not listening. Or perhaps it is true that men and women simply lose the ability to hear each other properly as they get older. Men lose high pitch, women lose hearing in the lower range. Maybe it's nature's way of keeping couples together. Except that my hearing is as accurate as my eyesight isn't and I had no choice but to listen.

'German nursing home, Christmas celebration, bring in the dancing bear. To entertain the old folks. Only it tripped on the wheel of some old *frau's* wheelchair. Sat on her. 200 kg.' He paused for another milky suck of his biscuit. 'What a way to go.'

I looked away to the hip-hip-hooraying. It died to leave words room. Words that shambled around the dining area. Words on a string, some missing as the mind failed to catch them as they floated free. Words trivial, words profound:

– my mother was born in 1886, she worked in a hotel, doing the breakfast trays, buttered toast wrapped in serviettes to keep it warm

– and then Benjy asked what had happened to Pop's head. Well, if they burnt the body, what happened to the head?

– oh, I only remember what I want. I pick and choose. What do I choose to forget? I don't know. I've forgotten

– I remember when our own Sovereign Lady Elizabeth was born

– our war was harder. Waiting for the men to come home. They never doubted they would. They thought they were immortal

– and he died at seventeen, my youngest, the Police car lost control in a chase. He was in the wrong place at the wrong time

– life? Eating, mating, avoiding danger, that's it. That's all.

Too much talk, a storm of it, a morning tea of it, eddying amongst the tea cups. So many examples of tragedy to anecdote in one lifetime.

There'd been too many voices, too many names all morning. Too much more than the patter of Margaret Throsby interviewing someone interesting on the radio. How would I ever get used to this Tower of Babel? The voices, the talking, so disjointed. Would it be anymore *jointed* if I settled down to one conversation—or still all angles and tangents disrupting a gentle flow, downhill, with gravity.

No, I was too used to my home and my magpies who rarely talked back. I was drowning. And I knew I would have sounded out just as much gibberish if I'd dared speak even once in the common room and not acted like a scared five year old on the first day of school who has lost all use of words, let alone the individual names of spoons.

Mavis smiled over the carnage of her cake. I was handed a piece. It was light and fluffy. The sugar revived me. I smiled back across at Mavis. Mrs. Balbilini I'd have to call her. She was my mother's age, had she lived of course.

My guide then reappeared to ask if I'd like to see one of the rooms.

'Come in if you're good looking,' called a brave voice from behind the first door she knocked on.

'Sorry, Mr Wright. I'll find a room that's empty.'

The next one was. A pretty room. A big window. Bushes outside. A hint of colour. Nice carpet, without threadbare patches, a china cabinet on one wall—'you can bring in some of your own furniture'—a pleasant, even temperature, a made bed, a reading light, a television. No doilies. No need to have doilies just because we're old.

It was a relief all round.

'And last ...' My guide hovered over the word, then let it go. 'Then we have the ward, for when you need the maximum care. Years off for you,' she laughed. It was impossible to say if she was sincere or being kind.

But even the ward was airy. An under-smell of disinfectant but no overwhelming cabbage and faeces pungency so easy to imagine. The air smelled instead of efficiency.

'Goodbye Mr North,' said one of the efficient nurses as a slight reed of a man stood up from beside a bed and made to leave. His returning smile was resigned.

The old woman in the bed called loudly, 'Nurse, why does the gardener keep coming to sit with me?'

'It's okay Mrs North. It's okay.'

'Yes, it's okay,' repeated my guide upon seeing my face. 'Mrs North always asks that.'

Does *always* failing to recognise your husband make it okay?

So this was it then. I took in every line on Mrs. North's face. So this was when it was too late. When the gas would be left on; and the bath runs so hot the burns would kill; and the wandering was no longer a worry but a mortal danger.

I needed to think. Time to breathe. There'd been too many impressions, first, second, third, lasting. The brain was talking, the gut contradicting. This was not simply finding a balance between a single bed with fresh linen and the empty double with pillows lined down one side, inadequate compensation for the absence there. A balance between fresh painted walls without traces of cockroach excrement, and the smell of Bob's aftershave and deodorant, even now, as I click open our wardrobe. Soon, I will not know that any of these things are gone. I won't know I have lost anything, once I've lost it all: once my safety net of memories is so gaping with holes that all thoughts, words and ideas slip through. I'll have to have another safety net, however many morning teas I have to sit through ...

If I could only keep things going—cobble it together, hobble it along.

'I need time,' I told my guide, truthfully, out in the corridor.

'Of course.' She was very kind. They were all very kind, and no one had called me dear all morning.

The closer I got to the front door of the place the better I felt. I'd put the kettle on when I got home, make a pot, settle down. And not think for a while. The horns of this dilemma were too sharp without a good lie down.

My sense of humour was even coming back as I got closer to the door. The horns of my dilemma: unfortunately I was not dealing with a unicorn, or even a cow; it was an aged multi-antlered stag I pictured. A foolish image, but humour is like spraying WD40 into the joints of a bike and it put some momentum into my step.

I'd decide tomorrow, I decided. Or the next day.

Only, is it indecision or rashness which has caused the most mistakes in life? I knew what the *right* decision was, of course. *Before it's too late,* echoed around and around as my guide disappeared behind the reception desk to unlock the front doors by remote. All newfangled and electric and secure security systems. All the right terms for them are in the brochure, I'm sure. It's a protection. No-one can get in, the paranoid who see the man in the bushes are assured. No-one can get out. If they're not supposed to.

It wasn't until I stepped into the square of sunlight falling through the glass doors that I spotted her—ridiculously camouflaged behind a potted fern. She had a black scarf tied under her chin, and a black handbag grasped in both hands.

I heard the click of the lock opening. So did she. She moved toward me. Slowly, so as not to draw attention? Slowly, because her legs gave no other option? 'I've got to go home,' she muttered in a thick Slavonic accent, her eyes on her feet, not on me, or the door, or freedom.

A glance back at the reception desk revealed my guide in conversation with one of the nurses. The door opened under the push of my shoulder but I kept the way barred with my body. But then the old woman stuck her foot out into the gap so I couldn't close the door back on her.

Still no one had noticed. Still she did not meet my eyes, still she did not move her foot. I could smell talc, inappropriately English Rose from under the widow's weeds. Should I push through, shove her foot aside? Or should I dawdle at the door—give her time to creep out? Old women are expected to doddle, dawdle, dither, it wouldn't look so suspicious.

'I've got to go home,' she said in monotone.

'I've got to go home too,' I complained. I think I sounded plaintive.

Her shoe was so old it was creased into the permanent shape of her foot. The heel and toes were scuffed. A lived-in shoe. Made for walking.

An old wives' tale from Russia says a dying person records on her eyes the last image seen. This old wife seemed to know what she wanted that to be.

'I've got to go home,' she said under her breath.

I wondered if she knew where *home* was now.

'It's all right. It's okay,' came an urgently gentle voice from behind. My guide had come to take her back. 'Come away, Mrs Kovacevic, come away dear.'

I was let through the door.

So now I have to make the right decision, you see. And I haven't got all day at all.

Jane Downing has had over ninety short stories published in Australia and abroad, and a similar number of poems. Her two novels, *The Trickster* (2003) and *The Lost Tribe* (2005), were published by Pandanus Books.

MARY MACPHERSON

REALITY SHOW

Rooftops, I've come up to play!
There's jazz fizzing on your edges
and ledges and the music swoops
round the façades' painted flourishes.
The freedom of the sky flares
above you—horn section in full flight—
while your surfaces switch from flat black
asphalt to fake grass, quick as a leap
over an alleyway. From up here, my gaze zips
down a building's concrete sides, skipping past
windows to miniature streets crammed
with lolly coloured cars and moving people
then grazes the knot of giggling girls
and the naughty afternoon woman sipping
red wine in the street
like it was her own reality show. People
on the ground fret on their tiny phones
but from the tall building planted
in a past century, I see each person's
journey as a fabulous story told
entirely in the present tense—like gazing
upwards at the breaking
news of clouds.

MARY MACPHERSON is a poet and photographer living in Wellington, New Zealand. In 2006 she completed an MA in Creative Writing at Victoria University. Her previous publications are the joint collection *Millionaire's Shortbread* (2003) and *The Inland Eye* (1998).

Grubby Love

Richard Lawson

She lives in Searle Street in Newtown, in the inner-city of Sydney. From the outside, her home is just another terrace, one more blistered façade the yuppies haven't got around to doing up yet. Inside, however, are clues that she's different: the Gay Pride flag draped above the door, the lamp-lit hallway festooned with photos. The hall is a floor to ceiling clutter of connections—her two boys, two girls, their partners, her grandkids, the relos, the strays. The strays—mainly dogs, but some humans too—steal most of the space. At the end, quietly framed, apart, is the photo of her Dad, decked in khaki, wearing his crooked smile under a Captain's cap. She's told he was a rascal, whatever that means. The scratched floorboards are mined with mauled pig ears, splintered bones, saliva-drenched cuddlies. The living room rug is lost under dog and cat hair. It's everywhere, under furniture, on top of the dining room table, in between her sheets. Even the walls are hairy. When she airs the place, matted wisps drift from room to room, like furry ghosts. Love, she likes to say, is a wondrous, grubby thing.

Her four-legged children, two dogs, two cats, are all poundlings, the results of rigorous, unnatural selection, chosen for the flaws that guaranteed they'd be chosen by nobody else.

Her first cat, Popeye, is jelly bean shaped, with a patch of black fur over his left eye, the blind one, which makes him look like a pirate. His heart is too big, his urinary tract plays up, and he shouldn't be alive. The fact, if he knows it, doesn't fuss him. He picks fights with flies and always loses. When he bounces home for his evening feed, there are scratches if he's lucky, an abscess if he's not. He's her baby and knows it. When he starts to beat up Karl, though, she draws the line—his cue to flop on his back, wiggle his shoulders lewdly, like he's doing a shoot for *Penthouse* (*her* cue to forget about drawing lines and tickle his tum.)

Her other cat, Mitsy, thinks she's the Queen of Sheba. Now her leg's mended, she occasionally leaves her throne on the kitchen benchtop and treats the bedrooms to a royal tour. When her mistress isn't looking, she forgets her blue blood and beats up Karl.

Gretel, the younger German shepherd, is a love-hungry destroyer. Physically she'd be perfect, but for the tooth she broke in a joust with the Hills Hoist out back. She lives for simple pleasures: food, vacuumed up before the spoon's out of her bowl, her afternoon howl-off with Rhonda the ridgeback next door, beating up Karl, the weekly trips to the dog run. She's calmed down a bit in the two months since her rescue. Obedience School is helping. Sort of. Only sometimes does furniture go crashing, or does she knock herself out while ramming the wall.

Last, but always first, is Karl. She'll deny he's the favourite, insisting she loves each animal differently but always equally. No one's fooled. He looks like a wolf but has the heart of a lamb. From behind the front window's curtain, his Cerberus bark knocks over passers by, but he's under the bed as soon as visitors cross the threshold. It's the same when thunder grumbles, or drug-happy yells ripple down from King Street, the centre of Newtown. Once, when fireworks were going off in the local park, he pushed out a rotting plank in the back fence and bolted all the way to Croydon, eight kilometres away, stopping only when his paw pads were raw. All her pets are high maintenance, but none have reached this altitude. He's a fixture bolted to her life, all the same.

Things might have been different. At the pound, helping her daughter pick a stray for the new house, she'd spotted him at once, cowering in one of the pens, crying out for saving. But things were just too tight, with interest rates rising and Mitsy's operation still to be paid off. That night, however, she dreamed of him atop a mountain of murdered dogs, waiting to be burned. She brought him home next day. Only temporary, she reminded herself in the car, until the right family came along. But when she opened the front door and tried to lead him inside, he dug in his paws and hosed the step with wee. She bent down, kissed his nose and held him, knowing already she'd never let him go.

He'll always be a mummy's boy. At the dog run, while the other dogs roughhouse, he peeks his nose mournfully from round the back of her legs, waiting hopelessly for an invitation to play. Lately, he's begun to venture away from her, one step, sometimes two, before the bounders rumble him, send him whimpering back behind her jeans. She measures his gains in notches so small only a mother can see them. The dog shrink is doing him wonders, she tells her dog friends. They smile to hide dissent, fond of her, and understanding the lies a parent must tell.

Her daughter's gone back up north to Brisbane now, to rejoin the clan. She misses her kids and their little ones, but she's allergic to Queensland. Just thinking of the bad old Bjelke Petersen days twists her gut. The National Party? National Socialist more like it! She filed for divorce and fled back south fifteen years ago, as soon as the kids moved out. She's never looked back. The kids say it's different now, under the new Labor government. She knows it ain't. She'll stay in Searle Street with her misfits, thanks all the same, till they put her in her box. Only occasionally she spits the dummy, when Gretel's tail upends her glass of red, or Mitsy sits on the keyboard just as she starts to email.

Hundreds of her emails clog the computers of the supposedly Honourable members of federal parliament, asking when, for a change, there's going to be a fair go for asylum-seeking children in detention, Iraqi civilians, workers, women—come to think of it, for all creatures great and small. She was one of the very few Newtown locals to vote *for* the heroin injection room next to the station. 'My backyard is as good as anyone else's,' she told the outraged residents at the emergency meeting.

She's getting more militant by the day. At Labor Party meetings she sits in the back row, wearing her Maritime Union of Australia T-shirt, slightly torn. Her motions are infamous—motions to sack the parliamentary leader, the shadow cabinet, the whole damned party, motions to blacklist America, free Palestine, call a General Strike, give Australia back to those it belongs to. They never pass. The local power brokers humour her, though. Whatever else, she's a giver. Come polling day, they know volunteers will be thin on the ground.

She never got past Fourth Form (women didn't back then, did they?) but like all self-taughts, she's a haphazard glutton for words. One day, she tells herself, when the dust has settled and justice been done, she'll start that novel about Dad.

There aren't any men in her life, not since she ended it with Bjorn, her merchant seaman, who drifted into and out of her life for fifteen years, giving a month of passion then leaving her to wait for a month, pretending not to.

She doesn't miss *them*, especially since things were fizzling in the bedroom. A fifteen-year holding pattern, that's what they amounted to, she's decided, though she still has a soft thought for him when she's mellow. She *does* miss the sex. Bjorn was always passionate, and these days there's Viagra. Even so, she's getting on. The body isn't everything anymore. From here on, she'll stick with animals—no passion, but the company is better.

Her arthritis bugs her, and the RSI flares up now and then. She can't afford to stop typing, though she'd like to retire. There's twenty thousand still on the mortgage and only a molehill of super. Saving's tough with Popeye's heart tablets, the animals' food, the vet bills, the monthly donations to RSPCA, Médecins Sans Frontières, Children by Choice, UNICEF. Soon there will have to be choices. She might have to give up the fags.

She'll manage all the same, so long as the animals warm her feet at night. And there's Bach, and books to read, and eyes to read with, not to forget politicians to harass, and ad-free public television (touch wood), and Newtown to keep her young.

Newtown will always be *her* town. She loves the way nothing here meets at ninety degrees. In the watering holes on King Street, she likes to wet her whistle and study the wildlife. They confirm all her stereotypes and confound them too. In recent years, though, the native species—Aborigine, Feral, Goth, Art Student—have been losing their habitat to the exotic yuppie. Rent hikes have driven the students to virtual extinction. A few persist in the last grunge cafes, blowing smoke, pretending to read Camus, acting like they just invented the human condition, but it's only a matter of time before they, with the other natives, vanish for good. Soon it'll be four-wheel drives, wine bars and nothing else.

The money hasn't driven away the sleaze though, just upped its price. The pubs still swill trashed patrons down her street, only later. And she still cleans spew and condoms from her pathway, only more often. And the old Hub, the iconic porno theatre next to the Town Hall, might be boarded up now, but sex shops on King are breaking out like herpes. It pains her to see men and women looking for empowerment and love in all the wrong places, but she can't march for tolerance and then get picky, can she? When she sees gays, dykes, straights, behaving badly side by side (if not hand in hand), or looks up at the King Street mural of Martin Luther King, she remembers the Nationals in Queensland and why she's here. Even so, more than ever, while money talks, it's poverty that walks. The beggars are slowly being pushed out of sight and mind. She notices how tolerance is spelt with a .com after it now.

Some days, to be sure, she wonders which planet the young ones come from. She watches boys dress like hobos, treat women like whores. And women dress like whores and treat boys, well, like girls. She hears the girls at the dog run counting scalps, rating lays, talking about love like it's war. It makes her grumpy, seeing her streets sick with all this choice and spin, while somewhere else, there's another world, but still her world too, which quietly starves. These are the days that Newtown makes her feel tired.

Then she remembers how she used to root like a rabbit too. How love has *always* been a war, just with different rules of engagement. Then she sees the old hippies playing Dylan CDs in their four-wheel-drives, or jogging in corporate T-shirts, and can't blame the young ones for losing their way.

Sometimes, she likes to ignore her sore bones, wander down King Street gazing upwards. The old facades are dated 1895 ... 1914 ... 1995. She wonders what the next fifteen years will bring, marvelling at the perverse, beautiful tenacity of life.

For her, though, the true leveller is the dog run in the nearby suburb of Haberfield. It's 500 by 100 metres of trampled grass, where difference is everywhere and nothing at all. Every Sunday she takes the shepherds. The place is rank with pooches—pure breeds, mongrels, in betweens: Beagles and Snoodles, Shih-Tzus and Chow Chows, Schnauzers and Shar-Peis, Rotties and Ridgebacks, Irish Wolfhounds, Norwegian Elkhounds, all the rest. Unleashed, they go berserk, in packs, solo, stealing each other's balls, tug of warring sticks, wrestling in the bindies, mad and free. Their wary parents hover under the trees, waiting for inevitable punch-ups. The parents come in all breeds, too, though divisions melt when they start talking things that matter—updates on Zeus's tail, advice on the best flea powder, Sandy's diet for watery stools, should Mel have snipped young Toro.

It tops her week. Owners and dogs, they're all extended family. Sometimes, the two-legged ones spill their secrets to her, stroking Karl. They tell her about Simon's relapse, asking her how they tell an eight-year old a truth they can't even tell themselves. They tell her how hard it is to date when you're forty, still in love with your wife, who's someone else's wife now and having his second kid. They tell how it'd be nice not to be twenty stone and dateless. They tell her, too, how it's almost okay til the light goes off, and that silence hits them so loud they want to die.

She doesn't say much, just listens, while they talk until they don't need to talk anymore. Sometimes, before they're done, someone spies Gretel taking a squat and hollers. They watch her scurry over the grass, pooper-scooper in hand, and feel glad the spell is broken, though glad as well to have it off their chests.

When the dogs are run ragged, everyone moves to the outdoor café *Bones*, where it's cappuccinos for two legs, puppuccinos for four. It's here, gossing with Sal, the vet nurse from the RSPCA shelter, that she hears about him first. Someone found him hopping around a deceased estate in Brown Street, brought him in, traumatised and starving. One back leg has been lifted by matted fur and bound to his stomach. Sal says they've fed him and cleared the gunk from his eyes, but he'll have to be put down. He'll need a general to cut the leg free, and what's the point? They'll never find him a home.

She drops off the dogs, drives straight to the shelter. Everyone there knows her, of course, smiles when she asks to see him. He's the sorriest excuse for a cat she's ever seen. She runs a hand over his coat, felted like a

Rasta's dreads. She winces when she gets to his ribs. She names him on the spot. Esky—for Every Sickness Known Yet. Once she's given him a name, she figures she has to give him a future. She takes him to her vet, Vera, and tells her to free the leg and do the necessary tests—she'll pay. Vera offers to do it for free, charging only cost price for the drugs. Her client is still paying off Mitsy's op from May.

She visits the pet shop, buys a cat cage, a shiny bowl, a pink rat. She bumps into Con, who announces Commodore, Falcon and Berlina all got places in Saturday's show. When she tells him about Esky, he turns beetroot with mirth. He's heard this before. He calls her Saint Jude, pretending to forget that atheists aren't allowed to be saints.

Back home, she pours herself a red, puts up her feet and lets it sink in. She can't explain why Esky's different, any more than she can tell why Karl was the one on that mountain she had to save. Is is is, as Mother used to say.

Vera rings Tuesday and enquires about Karl's ulcer. That's a bad sign. She asks about Esky's tests, expecting the worst.

'I'm sorry, love, we'll have to put him down. He's got feline AIDS.'

She makes Vera promise to wait, runs a red getting there but doesn't notice. When she sees the shaved bag of bones shivering on the slab, she kneels beside him and puts her face to his. She coos soft lies to his ear, strokes his paw. The needle goes in, reducing Esky, in seconds, to a melted heap. Vera gives her a hug, says the right things, but she doesn't hear. With all her pets, she's been through this a dozen times, but this feels horribly new.

She goes home and feeds her kids, because life goes on, doesn't it? Then she let's go, howls like all those years ago, after the beating she copped for hosing her stepfather, Ian. When she comes to, there is an empty wine bottle on the floor and the image of Esky in her mind, dumped in Vera's bin along with soiled bandages and kitty litter.

She sits there, tranced, sifting through her childhood—life before her life began. She remembers the welts from Ian's beating, wondering how she ever had the guts to hose him, wondering how welts can still burn fifty years on.

Then she remembers Mother, buying her a toffee apple from the corner store near their house. Maybe it's her birthday, or there's just been grief with Ian. She's crunching loudly, thinking Mother's happy, wondering how to make it last. Then she kisses the cheek, leaving an angry sore of candy goo and ruining everything. Mother doesn't like unscheduled kisses, or looking less than her best outside the house. It hurts when the spitted hanky starts yanking her fingers. She hears Mother's voice keeping time with each pull.

*'Dirty-Dirty-**Dirty**-Little-Girl!'*

When she returns to herself, she's on the edge of her bed, clutching the old biscuit tin. She opens it, coaxes out the brittle pages, covered with age spots, and sixty year old New Guinea mud. The letter—from Alfie Baynton, her dad's second in command—is addressed to Mother, of course. She reads what a larrikin, a leader, an all-rounder he was, and how often he spoke of the family. The last bit recounts his final morning: his good spirits, his rotten luck snagging a mine, the painless end. She reads it again, turning the words upside down, inside out, hoping for—not finding—something new.

She strips to her undies and kills the light. The animals are already hogging the bed. She squeezes in, lies still and listens. She hears the raucous silence of a jungle. She hears the deeper silence of sixty years waiting for his voice, waiting to know what she did to make him stay away. Finally, over the sound of Ian's belt hissing free of his pants, she hears the loudest silence of all, only a room, but a million miles away, where Mother turns up the radio, wipes off her make-up mask and cleans her pores.

RICHARD LAWSON has spent most of his working life teaching high school English. He has travelled through Asia, Turkey and Europe. Recently, he completed a law degree at the University of Technology, Sydney. He workshops his fiction every Friday night with a writers' group, finding these sessions both excruciating and invaluable. His short story, 'Portrait of an Artist as a Crumpled Horn,' was published in *Etchings 1*.

S. K. Kelen

Anthropology

The suburban approach to a youth's rite of passage
is more pleasant than a spear scraped across the chest
or a tunnel of paddles negotiated before the goat ride.
No elder should be in attendance. Every young punk
wants the first pash to be an epiphany (telling you
what you want to hear) so each new love leaves
further behind childhood's often noble soliloquy.
Once you've pashed a girl you'll understand
the world's delights, peaches and oysters
should always be there—each moment a kiss
of breath, the blood rises saying, 'it's great
to be alive'. Some, however, don't feel fulfilled
by a pash behind the tennis sheds, they need fast cars,
liquor, drugs, pain and thrills. They seek punishment.

FIREWORKS (KALI YUGA)

Rockets blaze the Sydney Harbour Bridge
smoke curls through holes
in the atmosphere, starbursts melt
phosphorescent waterfalls.
The harbour tempts:
restaurants, bars and dark places.
Kali and her slave, Lord Shiva, dance—
the many sweaty hands
hanging from her belt wave to passers-by.
The night sky lights up like an x-ray &
Midnight releases ancient energy: glitter sky,
toxic radiance exhilarates every spine—
Electricity—Kali comes & kisses
as Shiva eats her honeyed breasts.

S. K. KELEN is a Canberra-based poet who often teaches poetry and creative writing at the University of Canberra. His most recent books are *Goddess of Mercy* (Brandl & Schlesinger, 2002) and *Earthly Delights* (Pandanus Books, 2006). A volume of his new and selected poems will be published by Folio/Salt in 2007.

DREAMS AND REALITY
AN INTERVIEW WITH JOHN TRANTER

PATRICK ALLINGTON

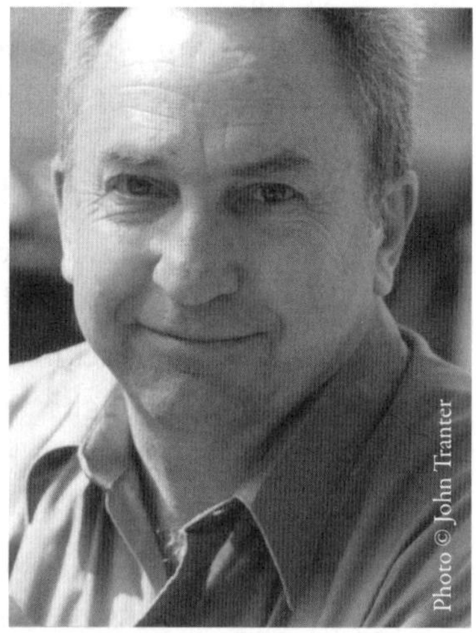

John Tranter, Berlin, 2002

John Tranter is one of Australia's most accomplished poets. His most recent book, *Urban Myths*, collects highlights from *Parallax* (1970) to *Studio Moon* (2003), and also includes previously uncollected poems and new work. *Urban Myths* won the 2006 CJ Dennis Prize for Poetry in the Victorian Premier's Literary Awards. John Tranter edited the controversial anthology *The New Australian Poetry* in 1979, and is the co-editor with Philip Mead of *The Penguin Book of Modern Australian Poetry* (1993). He is the founding editor of the groundbreaking online poetry magazine *Jacket*, which he produces from his home in Sydney.

What made you choose the title Urban Myths*?*

That was suggested to me by my wife, actually. I'd written a poem called 'Five Modern Myths', which is quite a popular poem, and I think that might have been in her mind. And, also, in the book *The Floor of Heaven* I have a number of long narrative poems, each of which contain some re-worked yarns that I'd heard when I was young and believed were true and then later realised weren't true—they were urban myths. I think it's a very intriguing area of research and discovery because urban myths are not constrained by any decorum, really. They can be as outrageous or as bizarre as you like and they don't seem to have an author, either, they just grow out of their community. So they're very strange things.

And in a sense I thought the word 'urban' was fair enough because I came to an urban environment from the bush, where I grew up, and I've always preferred to live in the city. And I think poems are like dreams, and dreams are like myths, in that they have some kind of archetypal structure and energy to them, even though we mightn't really know exactly how they work but we understand they have an importance of their own. So that's partly why I called it that—and it seemed like a nice title.

I detect a theme in your poetry that imagination, guess-work, half-knowledge, contribute to our forming of how we understand ourselves and our world. In that sense, urban myths, on a small scale, are all around us and we're living them.

I think it's quite fair enough to deduce that from the book. I guess poetry, like all art at its best, can help us understand the way we live from day to day ... I've always wondered what actual function poetry had. I can write poetry so I do—but *why* would anyone do it? What value does it have to society in the end? It seems if you analyse society and art and literature enough you come to understand that poetry is a kind of decoration at the edge of life. But I think it's actually more than that. Again, it comes back to this idea I have that the meaning of poems is a bit like the meaning of dreams. When you have an important dream it seems very intensely meaningful, although it's very hard to explain that to anyone who hasn't had the dream, and I think the meaning of poems are a bit like that. They're quite intense and meaningful and hard to explicate what the meaning is. And yet the meaning must have something to do with the way we live from day to day and what our lives mean. It's very hard to say what a human life means in the end, in the same way it is hard to explain what a poem means, and I think they operate on something like the same kind of level.

There's often a melancholic and resigned tone—but still hopefulness—in your poetry.

Well, yes, I'm aware of the fact that there are a lot of dichotomies in my writing. I'm very cynical at times in my poetry, which is partly the laconic mode that Australians use a lot but it's also there partly as a kind of balance to the sentimentality that I think I have a lot of but that I try to suppress because I think it's a bit gushy. So I'm aware of these two things also in balance in my work, or I hope they're balanced, and that's true of idealism on the one hand and negative despairing thoughts on the other. On the one hand we all have to die which is horrible but on the other hand we're all alive, which is wonderful.

That desire to stamp down on the sentimentality is quite overt at times ...

I think a lot of readers might not like it because they get carried away with an idea that is wonderful and then there's this deflating thing at the end and they might be disappointed at being treated like that, perhaps.

I think I like it for that precise reason—because the best idea is still just one idea.

Yes, that's true. I think partly that comes from my upbringing in the Australian bush where you were taught not to be too gushy about anything. Again, it's that laconic mode that Australians have a lot of. Whether that's good or bad I don't know but that's just the way it is. Because it's a particularly Australian thing I would think that most of my audience would understand it fairly easily.

Your early work was very much a challenge to the conservatism of existing Australian poetry. Your introduction to The New Australian Poetry *anthology (1979) now reads to me like a quite mild and measured piece of writing.*

At the time it was seen as being quite strange and energetic and people disliked it a lot. It was first actually delivered as a paper at a Macquarie University conference in 1974 called 'The American Model.' It was published in the magazine *New Poetry* soon after that and people who read it and disliked it were quite aggressive about it. I mean, there were things wrong with it: the scholarship was a little sloppy here and there and I think I over-explained things too much. But I was writing for a general readership in a sense. There's a good response to that anthology by Martin Harrison. He reads the anthology as something that was very much needed at the time and he thinks it's a good thing that it happened. So it was interesting to get that response from him. And I think when you look at that period of writing—say 1965 to 1975—it really was a period where the world of writing was divided between older writers and younger writers in a way much more so than had happened before or after that in Australia. There was a comparable wave of new poetry written in the 40s actually which is quite interesting to look at. Debut books by Judith Wright and Francis Webb and a whole lot of other writers. But with that particular wave of young writers there wasn't a feeling that they were fighting against an old guard, as it were, they just each produced a book and everyone said, 'Isn't that nice,' and they produced another book .... I sometimes worry which generation of writers younger writers are going to oppose these days, because the older generation are all experimentalists and let you do whatever you like.

Would you characterise yourself as a dissenter—then and/or now? What motivates you to write poetry now?

Young people these days ... they simply cannot be aware how dull and authoritarian and repressive Australian society was in the 1950s and 1960s. In the permissive present, it's impossible to feel or understand how awful it was then. Just to wear your hair a bit long was a statement: young Michael Dransfield was badly bashed in a street in King's Cross one evening just because of his long hair, bashed by ordinary Australian blokes whose parents would have approved of what they did: of course you bashed long-hairs, hippies and poofters, they're asking for it. I knew a woman whose father was persecuted by the police for years because he read banned books and was a communist. When I returned from the UK in 1967 I found that the customs service had confiscated and destroyed two paperback books I had sent ahead with my belongings in an old trunk. They were harmless works of literature, as far as I can recall. So being a poet, smoking dope, protesting against the draft and the Vietnam War, reading intellectual books, listening to loud rude rock music, engaging in sex before marriage—all of these things, we were made to feel, were foul and anti-social criminal acts. Of course you dissented. Unless you were Les Murray, who went along with the conservative pro-war, anti-hippie, anti-feminist rhetoric—it was good for his career, at that time, being James McAuley's protégé at *Quadrant,* a magazine funded by the CIA for many years. But most younger poets dissented.

So a general feeling of dissent energised much of the poetry and music and art of the late sixties. What motivates me to write poetry now, when all the noise and smoke of battle has faded away? Well, it's a mystery. John Forbes talked about his role as a poet, in an oblique way, in his great poem 'Monkey's Pride', like this: '... I'll be employed on a rowing boat / mounted in a park, / the one the avenues lead to / because society has elected me / to decorate / its falling apart / with a useless panache / & I will, / despite my vocation / to become a labour-saving device, opening / cans by remote control / in the kitchen of your heart / bottling the vegetables / you grow in your own backyard.' Somewhere between the bottling machine and the useless panache lies the task of the poet.

In some ways the greatest mystery in the history of poetry is the fact that Rimbaud gave up poetry when he was nineteen. In some ways the fact that I continue to write poetry, when I know quite well that the practice is useless, is a mystery rather like that. Not nearly as important as that, but in the same domain, and reversed.

Reading Urban Myths, *there's a real sense to me of your poetry being somehow 'quintessentially' Australian. What do you think of that notion?*

I don't seek to appear to be 'Australian', though I grew up on a farm and can drive tractors and shoot a shotgun and all that stuff. Unlike some poets, I don't have anything invested in that kind of role-playing. When

I was young I couldn't wait to grow up and leave the bush and go to the big city where people didn't gossip about you and the intersections had traffic lights. Three decades ago David Malouf told me that however internationalist I wished to be—and I was mouthing off about the need to escape parochialism at that time—I would always have an Australian tone of voice, an Australian accent, an Australian way of looking at things. He's right. I think it has something to do with the Laconic Mode, which is an oblique way of thinking and speaking that Australians naturally employ. I've been to New York twenty times, but I still call Australia home.

In contrast, Jacket *is a most international of magazines.*

With *Jacket*, I just try to publish the best and most varied and most interesting poetry I can find, and because *Jacket* appears (only) on the Internet and because the Internet has such a vast global reach, and because ninety-five per cent of the interesting poetry in the world is not Australian, *Jacket* reflects that and has very little Australian material, proportionately. It's not intentional; that's the way the world of poetry in English today happens to be. Of course if *Jacket* was ever afflicted with a Literature Board grant, I would be forced to change that, and make fifty per cent of the material Australian. Heaven forfend!

Jacket *is coming up to ten years. Most literary magazines don't come close to making it that far.*

That's right. A lot of them only last one or two issues. My magazine *Transit* only lasted two issues. Some go on too long: *Poetry Australia* and *New Poetry* both outlived their lifespan a little bit but that's okay. And *Scripsi* really lasted ten years and died too ... so it might be a good idea to close down at ten.

I think a lot of literary magazines, in print at least, start out with a particular constituency, mainly younger poets who want to present their view to the world as being different from that of older poets. I mean, if you don't have ideas that you think are completely different and important then you might as well just publish in the older magazines anyway. But if you want to start a new magazine it's because you've got a new idea or philosophy or a new movement you want to promote and those movements tend not to last more than a decade anyway. But I never really had a polemical purpose for *Jacket*. I didn't have a particular mission that I felt the magazine had to fulfil. In a sense it was just a compendium of anything I could find out there that was interesting to read and that I wanted to put in a magazine. It may last longer because of that.

One of the really appealing things about Jacket *is the range of poets covered, and the depth in which they are covered. I've noticed this particularly with the quite frequent 'in memoriam' features, such as the recent feature on the American poet Robert Creeley.*

Critics have sometimes implied that it is a bit gloomy, *Jacket's* featuring so many major elder poets as they drop off the perch, one by one ... a kind of literary death-watch beetle gnawing away in the wainscoting as the grandfather clock ticks in the shadowy corner. But it is a way of taking the opportunity of the light from that brief and final supernova glow of fame, a chance to make people aware of some great writers and read about them while their name is still in the news. It is also a chance for poets and critics to say how and why the recently-dead have mattered to them.

As it happened, I had planned the Creeley feature a year or so before he died unexpectedly, as I did with Kenneth Koch, whose illness was more apparent and more threatening. Creeley died just as I was in Philadelphia preparing to give a reading. I was impressed by how many of the people in the audience were deeply affected by the loss: mainly much younger people. We turned the first half of my reading into a memorial reading for Creeley, which felt like the right thing to do.

I should say that I don't feel the impact of his writing as strongly as younger American poets seem to; I had my own very various influences over many decades and for me Creeley was a peripheral influence, though of course he was a major poet. But for younger American poets, beleaguered and out of place in their materialistic mass society, he spoke clearly—in a very American tone of voice—for a personal and complete dedication to the poetic life, and even though he spent his life mainly as an academic teacher, he was never conservative in a dull scholarly sense. He represented a radical, alternative academia, and a very personal kind of scholasticism. After being thrown out of Harvard he went on to Black Mountain College, a radical left-leaning arts-oriented college, in the 1950s, and spent much of his later life teaching at SUNY Buffalo, also—for some decades—a somewhat intellectually adventurous place.

Mainstream publishers and mainstream booksellers seem to be in reasonably hasty retreat from poetry. Does that make the Net an important part of the future of poetry?

Yes, the problem with poetry is distribution. You can write poems, you can print them, you can make a magazine up without too much expense but to get them into New York or London is impossibly expensive. The Internet does that for nothing for you so you get immediate world-wide free distribution with the Net. And that solves the main problem that poetry's always had. That's always the nexus where you fall down with a print magazine but you don't have that problem. In fact you have the opposite on the Net: you have an audience out there that wants to find things that you have to offer and they'll come to you rather than you having to find them. I think I mentioned in an article about the Net, in the first issue I published an interview I'd done with the British poet, Roy Fisher. And I got a letter from a fellow thanking me for publishing it. He said 'I'm a great fan of Roy Fisher's and it's hard to find work on him up here at Nome, Alaska.'

In a sense, the rules of online publishing are different but they're not that *different.*

They're not that different. In fact, people in the early days of the Internet were saying, 'Oh, it's wonderful, we can do poems that move on the page, and that glow, and that disappear.' Well, you can do that, and some of them are extremely interesting, particularly using Flash technology.

There's a poem called 'the dreamlife of letters' by Brian Kim Stefans that's a wonderful example of letters and words that move about on the screen, it's just beautiful to look at. But that's distracting in a sense to me. I really see *Jacket* as an easy way of distributing a well-designed magazine and I'm not interested about the fact that it's on the Net or it's electronic or you can do this or that with the lettering.

One interesting complexity with writing on the Internet is the fact that anybody can post their work. Whatever the advantages of this, creatively there can be an element of quality control absent.

Well, that's where I'm lucky again in that I've been an editor all my life. ... There used to be an advertisement, 'It's the fish that John West reject that makes John West the best.' If you let everything in, no one wants to read what you're doing, in the end. There are places on the Net where anyone can get themselves published so it's not that I'm preventing people from getting into print. If they want to get into print they can do it all themselves just as I did with *Jacket* or my own homepage. But for the sake of my readers I want them only to find interesting material in *Jacket*. A lot of writers just don't think enough about what they're writing to be able to edit themselves.

Many new poets/writers still feeling their way, finding their voice, find the idea of an editor, and the process of editing, quite mysterious. Could you explain something of what it means to be a poetry editor?

I've been an editor for so long that it's become like walking: I really can't explain how I do it. I've copy-edited a giant tome called *Grasses for Sheep in Australia*; I've edited radio plays and poetry magazines and distance educational material and books on Southeast Asian sociology. I was browsing through the weekend papers the other day when I picked up a misspelling: 'we were plum set against it' instead of 'plumb set'; 'plumb' is from the Latin for the metal lead; a plumb-line (a piece of lead on a string) is what builders use to get an accurate vertical. Perhaps it was just a typo.

I revise a lot when I'm writing prose or poetry, and it's the revision that turns a moth-eaten sow's ear into the gleaming silk purses I'm known for.

(Just joking.) To me, editing is just another person kindly providing an extra layer of revision. It's important that books should be edited for the press, so the typesetting and syntax and spelling are all clean, and it's probably a good idea that poems should be edited to improve them, though that hardly ever happens.

That's one kind of editing: close editing, going over a text word by word and suggesting improvements. It's perhaps the kind of thing a musician might do in a Master Class.

Then there's the work I have done compiling poetry anthologies, which is a quite different kind of editing. In that situation you can't do much to improve what's on offer. You just select the good bits and throw out the bad. And of course you want to balance the overall shape of the thing, and counter-balance one kind of poetry with another, and perhaps throw in a prose-poem for contrast, and place an angry poem next to a peaceful poem, and perhaps contrast a supportive, questioning tone of voice with a judgmental, aggressive tone of voice, and so on. Like writing poetry itself, you have to have a natural talent for it—as a potential musician needs to have been born with perfect pitch and the ability to carry a tune—and then you also need years of study and training, as a painter or a pianist or a surgeon does. But when I look at a poem it feels like an instinct at work, not a process of careful intellection: I know straight away how the poem works, and what's good and what's not so good about it. To put it another way, I once showed John Forbes a poem I'd been working on for a day or two, and was rather pleased with. He glanced at it briefly and handed it back, with the comment 'The last line's fucked, mate.' Which it was: I deleted it.

A longer version of this interview, along with a bibliographic essay, is available at www.ilurapress.com

Tammy Ho Lai-ming

Scent

How do you smell now?
The scent used to cover
the entire washroom,
my entire lungs.
It sneaked out of your fingers.
It combed the hair on your arms.
I saw it last under the bedclothes.

Where is it now?
I look for it in the books you bought me.
But between the pages
I only find sighs
and cloudy images of you
sulkily opening a bottle of wine.

What does wine taste like?
It used to taste of sweet Saturdays,
a bunch of pearly smiles,
lingering kisses on your shirt collar.
When we drank wine
you wrote a love letter on my bare thighs.
When we drank wine
I was attracted to
your gentle and puzzling neck.

How is your neck now?
I tried to iron its creases
with my tongue.

And your tongue, how is it now?
Is it still so cute
and good at penetrating.

TAMMY HO LAI-MING, aka Sighming, is a Hong Kong-born and -based writer. She writes about what makes the world a landscape of anguish and gratification: love, life and lust. More at www.sighming.com

Ouyang Yu

The Kingsbury Tales: Ways of Not Telling the Stories

In Kingsbury, the deadest of all the dead places in this dead country
One occasionally learns ways of not telling the stories

For example, when Ru Yu and Rong Lu have an affair
And make love, Lei, their author, dismisses it by saying:

They are doing this sort of embarrassing thing that offends
Public morals but I don't have to dirty my pen in writing about it[1]

Similarly, when Wang Qi pushes Yu Na, a dancing girl, onto her bed
Lei says he did not see what they did subsequently and so had to skip it[2]

What Lei stopped writing about 4 decades ago one can probably pick up
And expand upon now but, then, will Australian readers understand?

In this equally prudish age, one can probably do what Zhang did in 1906
When he said he did not explain what comforting words Lu, a prostitute

Said in the ear of her estranged client, Ma, because he
"did not hear what was said and cannot just make it all up

and have to leave my readers to figure it out and imagine it all"[3]
Now, to borrow their technique of not telling you the story

I decide to leave the rest
Such as how the entire novel is centred around one man consorting

With multiple prostitutes and how he makes love with the underaged
To your imagination as well, in Kingsbury, in the dead early 21st century

---

1 Lei Zhusheng, *hai shang huo di yu* (Hell Alive at Sea), published by Chunfeng Publishing House, 1997 [1929], p. 44.

2 Ibid, p. 70.

3 Zhang Chunfan, *jiu wei gui* (The Nine-tailed Turtle), published by People's China Publishing House, 1993[1906], Vol., III, p. 817.

OUYANG YU has published 36 books of poetry, fiction, literary translation and literary criticism in both Chinese and English. He is now the Chair Professor of Australian Literature in the English Department, Wuhan University, China. He has won a number of literary awards, including the 2004 South Australian Festival Award for Innovation in Fiction for his novel, *The Eastern Slope Chronicle*. Ouyang Yu can be visited online at www.ouyangyu.com.au.

Fat of the Land
Extracts from a Novel

Andrea McNicoll

1. The Widow Ghost

I

'Another shot, Uncle Nun?' Lai leaned over his bamboo bar, rubbing the glasses with an old cloth.

'Nah, Lai. S'time for bed. Where's everyone gone tonight anyway?' Uncle Nun swung his arm out at the village behind him, almost toppling his stool.

'Oh, those poor men with wives, Uncle Nun.' Lai yawned dryly.

Wife won't be back for another two months, Uncle Nun had boasted earlier to his cronies, pointing to his chest with his thumb. Until then I can please myself. Ha ha!

'Poor men. I'll say. Guess I'll be off home too, Lai. Be seeing you tomorrow.'

'Sweet dreams, Uncle Nun.'

Uncle Nun climbed down carefully from the stool, which felt higher than usual. Immune to the cool air, he walked unsteadily along the road, empty now except for a few dogs curled up on the tarmac, lifting their snouts and growling as he staggered past. Most of the houses were in darkness, just the odd light still on. His place was at the end of the street, the last house in the village before the rice fields. There we go—one, two, three, oops, ha ha—up the steps. He opened the front door, switching on the light. Bright. Two shiny cockroaches scattered in opposite directions across the dirty floor; one disappeared under the fridge, the other between the wooden boards. Oh, what the hell, Uncle Nun giggled, opening the fridge for some water, wrinkling his nose at the smell as if it was someone else's fault. The shelves were empty except for a few bottles of water, a shrivelled half lime, a nub of galangal, furry and blue round the edges. Food from the market was easiest these days. Rice and curry for breakfast, noodles at twelve from Aunty Wassana's stall, fried chicken with chilli paste and sticky rice most nights. And a few glasses of moonshine. What more could a man ask for? Uncle Nun shrugged. Not that he couldn't cook, of course. His jungle stew was legendary. He made it every year on his birthday. Legendary was the word, his wife said, a legendary mess in the kitchen to clean up. What did she know?

The only problem with market food was indigestion. The doctor had told him to avoid anything too spicy. Ulcer or something. He belched and rubbed his stomach with one hand, rustling with the other on the top of the fridge. Where did she keep the Chinese medicine? Why were women always hiding things? Ach, might as well go to bed. Look for it in the morning. He stumbled into the bedroom and swayed. The bed sheets were crumpled. The mosquito net had been lying open all day. He pulled his shirt over his head without undoing the buttons, let it fall, and sank down, tucking the net around the bed, sighing. Lots of room to stretch out now he was on his own. He rolled over to his wife's side, sniffing her pillow, the faint smell of talcum powder and face cream. He turned over on to his back, feeling the familiar acid rise in his throat. He belched and closed his eyes. A mosquito buzzed, biting his leg. Uncle Nun slapped at it, yawned noisily, and fell into another night of fitful sleep.

He had gone to sleep on his back, snoring. Had dreamt his wife was poking his ribs to make him turn over and shut up. Uncle Nun rubbed his eyes and looked over at the bedroom window, the shutters open to let the night breeze blow cool. He blinked. A white shape seemed to shine in the darkness outside. The moon? His eyes opened wider. Not the moon. The shape grew larger, more distinct. What was it? It looked like ... yes ... it was a young woman, moving in the night air towards the window, floating inside, tiny feet barely resting on the wooden floor. She gazed at him from the corner of the room for a moment, her beautiful head on one side, then drifted over to his bed, pulling back the mosquito net. Uncle Nun was transfixed. She knelt down and reached inside, stroking the side of his head with her pale, cool fingertips. A delicious heaviness overwhelmed his limbs, pinning him to the sheets. The woman's slim body was barely covered by a thin nightdress. Her long black hair brushed his naked chest as she leant over him. He could smell frangipani blossoms. She smiled with full red lips, showing perfectly formed little teeth, and whispered tender words in Uncle Nun's ear, words long forgotten, words his mother had soothed him to sleep with, uttered in the same velvet accents he had once used with his young wife on their wedding night. Then, stirred into a deep yearning by his memories, he gripped her naked arm and looked into her eyes where he saw naked, grinning lust. She hitched up her thin nightdress, moved her pale thighs apart and made to straddle him—*straddle him*, mind you—and it was only then Uncle Nun came to his senses. He pushed the most unnatural female aside, jumped up, fumbling out from the mosquito net, running out of the bedroom, out the house and into the breaking dawn, covered in sweat, in bare feet and old trousers.

'A widow ghost!' he cried out to the startled villagers on their way to the morning market. 'A widow ghost has tried to steal my soul.'

II

Since the morning of Uncle Nun's announcement, the village had been in turmoil. Rumours abounded. At first the ghost was seen once a week, then every night. It came from a darkly evil place somewhere beyond the valley, behind the mountains, far from the village. It flew in high over rice fields, low through the village streets, in and out of the deserted stalls in the morning market. Uncle Daeng claimed to have heard it whooping over the field behind his house, stealing across the backyards. Mother Nong whispered to her neighbours how she had found its bloody fingertips on her husband's laundry, left out on the washing line. It upturned vegetable baskets, scattered children's toys. The widow ghost, said the Chinese grocer's wife, had withered the tiny chillies on the bushes in her garden. And Sergeant Yud, after a night duty, told how he had covered his ears, huddling with the prisoners in their cell to escape the hideous swallowing sound of the ghost, clearly desperate with hunger, as it drank the blood of the old dog that slept behind the police station. The dog had been found dead in the morning, eyes glassy, fur rigid with fear. Mosquitoes got under tightly closed nets, glasses and plates were inexplicably dropped and smashed, rice and curry were spilled on floors, attracting armies of ants, and the noon breeze blew hotter than ever before. All the fault of the widow ghost. Children screamed, mothers wept, farmers furrowed their brows. Something, thought the Abbot, would have to be done. He sat in the temple, cross-legged in the main hall, hands upturned in his lap, trying to make sense of it all.

The single men in the village, of whom there were an increasing number these days, were the most afraid. They knew the widow ghost had come particularly for them. And there was little the Abbot could do to help. Uncle Nun had been the first to visit, kneeling in front of him with an uncommonly large offering of mangoes, lychees, lotus buds and an envelope of money, pleading for an incantation, a prayer, a piece of magic cotton to wear around his wrist to ward off the wicked ghost and her desire. The Abbot had obliged with a standard Pali text, a sprinkling of holy water over Uncle Nun's head, and a piece of white cotton more sacred than magic. The Abbot didn't do magic. It was not his business and it had never before been part of his religious duties to deal with widow ghosts. He had read the texts over and over again and there was no mention of ghosts. And yet, with each day that passed, his line of male visitors grew longer and longer; he saw the young and old, the divorced and widowed, the available and the abandoned. All sought reassurance and protection from the ghost. All he could really offer them was advice and a blessing.

'Adhere to the Five Precepts. Make some merit. Keep your feet firmly on the Middle Path. Fill your head with righteous thoughts and your heart with compassion. *Saddhu, saddhu, saddhu*!'

The men were unconvinced. Frenzy about the ghost increased. There was more than one ghost, some said, a band of widow ghosts was roaming the countryside looking for men to seduce, kill and take as husbands. An old man chanced to die in his sleep. Was he the ghosts' latest victim? For guidance, the men turned impatiently from religion to the Shan fortune-teller. On his advice, wooden phalluses were hastily carved, and hung from the village gateposts and in almost every doorway to distract the ghosts. One farmer even made a pair of testicles from coconut shells, and wove pubic hair from an old fishing net. The authenticity of his phallus made him the envy of other men. Some men had even started wearing red nail polish to fool the widow ghosts into thinking they were women. Uncle Nun was seen wearing an old blouse his wife had left behind when she went to work in the city.

Games of poker were organised to last all night, ensuring the men were kept awake, together, safe from attack. Business at Lai's moonshine stall was particularly brisk. Even the most confirmed bachelors were looking for women to whom they might propose. But to whom? There had been a shortage of women, especially young women, in the village since Sia Heng, the local Chinese businessman, had invited his rich cousin to visit. The cousin had used the opportunity to recruit female workers for his fruit processing factory in the city. Apart from his managers, his workforce was composed entirely from women; he could pay them less and trust them more. Some married women had joined the recruitment drive, eager for a regular wage, and a chance to experience a little city life, a bit of independence. Fathers, brothers, even husbands were left to fend for themselves. The Abbot shook his head sadly. It wasn't right. The natural order had been upturned. He couldn't deal with this on his own. He sighed, deciding the only way forward was to speak to the village headman, and call a meeting of the elders.

III

The meeting was held in the temple's main hall. A semicircle of elders faced the Abbot, whose superior status allowed him to sit with his back to the Buddha statue. Portraits of the great, good Thai kings adorned one wall, a colourful mural of the Buddha's ten incarnations filled the length of the other. It was evening, still warm and sticky. Nature was slipping into the hot season, when tempers ran notoriously short. Electric fans on either side blew the mosquitoes off course, keeping the meeting's focus intact. The Abbot cleared his throat and began.

'Well, I don't need to tell you why we are here tonight. I am most perturbed by this, this ... attack,' the Abbot waved his wand absently, 'this so-called attack on the village by ... hmm ... ghosts.'

'Not just any old ghosts,' said the district officer, who had read a great many books on the subject. '*Widow* ghosts.'

'Oh, stuff and nonsense,' said the schoolmaster. 'There's no such thing as ghosts, widowed or otherwise. Who's actually seen this ghost, apart from Uncle Nun? Uncle Nun? Drunk as a skunk every day on moonshine. Ghost? Hallucinations, more like.'

'Well, the question is,' said the Abbot, eager to stop the meeting collapse into the usual bickering, 'how to allay everyone's fears about the ghost, real or imagined.'

The headman cleared his throat, took a deep breath. The other men cast their eyes heavenward.

'The problem of the widow ghost,' he began, 'reminds me of a problem I encountered in the year 2522, in the month of June. Or was it July? It may have been July. Indeed. At that time a similar excitement had taken hold of the village. Yes, a similar excitement. A vampire was purported to have attacked an old woman. What was her name? Let me see ... yes, Grandmother Rung. Grandmother Rung was very old, perhaps eighty, a very fine age to live to, if you ask me.' The headman paused to nod wisely, wagging his forefinger at the rest of the group. 'She was a healthy woman. Two boiled eggs every morning for breakfast. I remember her telling me. Two boiled eggs. That was her secret. Grandmother Rung never suffered a day's illness in her ...'

'Could we get to the point?' the schoolmaster interrupted.

'I was just getting to it,' huffed the headman. He was older than the schoolmaster and didn't take kindly to such disregard for his age and position. 'We decided to hold a merit-making ceremony to get rid of the vampire. We held a big ceremony. A *suepchada* ceremony. It worked. The vampire was never seen again. So I propose we do the same now.'

'Quite,' said the schoolmaster sarcastically. 'What do you think, Abbot?'

'Well, a merit-making ceremony can never be a bad thing. Brings the people together as a community, encourages them along the right path.'

'But aren't we going too far?' asked the schoolmaster. 'Surely, by arranging a ceremony, aren't we vindicating the ghost's existence? Is that wise? Does it not merely set a precedent for more scares, hauntings, strange sightings, and who knows what?'

The headman and the district officer winked at each other. They weren't entirely sure what the words 'vindicating' and 'precedent' meant. Such words were typical of the schoolmaster, who was originally from Bangkok. Even though he had lived in the village for twenty years, he still stuck to his central dialect. Highfalutin nonsense.

'Well, what's your suggestion then?' asked the district officer.

'We should examine the reasons behind such a frenzy. Why, grown men—carving penises, wearing wigs and nail polish. All because one drunken fool had a bad dream?'

The district officer coughed. His wife had gone to visit her mother, who lived in another village, a few weeks ago and was yet to return. Her absence, he felt, left him vulnerable to attack. Rather than take any chances, he had been going to bed dressed in his wife's nightgown, a big wooden phallus hanging above the front door.

'What reasons for the sightings could there possibly be?' interrupted Sia Heng.

None of the men were sure that Sia Heng should even be at the meeting. When had he become a village elder? Someone had invited him along just because he was rich and successful. The men looked around, each suspecting the other of inviting Sia Heng.

'Well,' said the Abbot, 'I can't help but wonder if the fact that so many of our women are absent might have something to do with it?'

'We've got Sia Heng to thank for that,' shouted the district officer, excited at finding a scapegoat. 'If you hadn't invited that cousin of yours with his fancy fruit processing factory to visit, there wouldn't be so many men without wives.'

'That's right,' said the village headman. 'It's hardly natural.'

'No wonder we are being attacked by widow ghosts. The ghosts are drawn to our village because so many men are on their own now,' concluded the district officer.

'Gentlemen, gentlemen, calm down.' The Abbot raised his hands, shaking his head sadly from side to side. It was always like this. He should have found a way to solve the problem by himself.

'Is it my fault if the village women want to leave and work in a factory?' asked Sia Heng. 'Surely the extra money they bring home can only improve their lives and the village economy? Since when was it wrong for people to leave home and contribute to the family purse?'

'Women though? It's not right,' said the headman. 'In the old days they stayed at home and we knew where they were, what they were doing. Women off alone in the city isn't right. Coming back home with ideas. I should know. Look at my daughter. Two years working in Bangkok and she won't listen to me anymore. Doesn't want to get married, even though she's twenty-three now. Drinks beer and smokes cigarettes. Spends half her money on clothes and going to the cinema.'

'And it's anyone's guess what these girls get up to with young men in the city,' said the district officer, fanning his red face with a folded newspaper.

'For goodness sake,' shouted the schoolmaster, 'this is supposed to be the modern age, isn't it?'

'*Modern*?' sneered the district officer. 'Is that what you *city* people call staying out all night and sleeping around?'

At that the schoolmaster made to get up, reminding himself just in time to bow three times to the Buddha statue before leaving.

'Oh, do whatever you like. Have your *suepchada* ceremony if it makes you feel any better.'

'It's all very well for him,' said the district officer, watching him go. 'He's got a wife for protection. What about the rest of us? It's our civic duty to protect those most at risk!'

'I second the idea of a merit-making ceremony, and I'm willing personally to meet the majority of the costs,' said Sia Heng, knowing his generosity would greatly improve his social standing in the village.

'Why that's most generous of you, Sia,' said the headman. 'And we haven't forgotten it was you who paid for the new temple roof.'

'Quite, most generous,' said the Abbot, eager to bring the matter to some sort of close. 'We all agree then a merit-making ceremony is the best way forward?'

The district officer nodded, happy with the idea of a ceremony paid for by Sia Heng, which would, after all, be an excuse for a big party. The women working away in the fruit processing factory might even be able to come home for it, said the headman. Sia Heng would speak to his cousin about it, and everyone would be happy then. They would need the women home anyway, added the Abbot, to prepare the food. He found it most comforting to think that many of his regular alms-givers would be back for a few days. The monks and novices could therefore look forward to something more substantial than the instant noodles they had recently been forced to rely on.

IV

'Hey Lai, set me up another round!' said Sergeant Yud, red-faced.

'"Eleven Tigers" or "Widow Ghost?"' asked Lai, pointing to the different coloured bell jars behind him.

'Oh, make it a "Widow Ghost." And wait till you hear what Sergeant Pan dreamed the other night after a few glasses of your new blend.'

Lai laughed. The new mixture had become a great favourite.

'Still no sign of Uncle Nun then?' asked the Sergeant, peering down the road.

'Not since the ceremony.'

The ceremony had been a great success. Everyone felt much more comfortable as a result. It was unlikely the village would be attacked again now it had shored up on its store of merit. The farmers were convinced it would help the rains start a little earlier too. They could look forward to a bumper rice crop. The other bonus was that many of the women who had come back to take part in the ceremony had been persuaded to stay on. The days of widow ghosts, it would seem, had passed.

Even Uncle Nun wasn't sure anymore whether he had actually seen or just dreamt about the beautiful woman and her strange appetites. He leant over his balcony, straining his neck to see Lai's stall at the other end of the road. He could just make out the bulk of Sergeant Yud, perched on a stool. He'd be on his third or fourth glass by now. Uncle Nun licked his lips wistfully.

'Nun. Nun. Come in and get your dinner.'

'What're we having tonight then? Aw, not rice porridge again. Woman, can't you cook proper food anymore?'

'Do you want to get better or not? You know what the doctor said. And there'll be no going off to the whisky stall afterwards either.'

At that, Uncle Nun shook his head sadly, and went indoors.

2. The Sword

I

It was not as though Mother Pensri had never seen foreigners; she saw them every Saturday night on Channel 7. But the American films Uncle Nun, her husband, loved to watch were all dubbed into Thai, so the actors' mouths moved uncomfortably out of sequence to the words. She had the vague feeling there was something suspicious about them—as though they couldn't possibly mean what they seemed to be saying. Too much running around and shouting, waving guns, undressing and kissing, for her liking. But the foreign actors were certainly better looking than most of the real *farangs* she had seen in Chiang Mai. They came up from Bangkok and the south to visit the famous northern capital, to buy silks and souvenirs at the night bazaar, to wonder at the ancient temples, to smack their lips at the excellent food. Their bare white arms, fleshy shoulders and plump legs enthralled her, as did the way they strode around in the hot sunshine even though they could, she presumed, so easily afford to hire a taxi or a *tuk tuk*.

Over the last year or so, *farangs* had even started to venture as far as the village, especially in the winter months when the weather was dry and cool.

They took pictures of the rice fields, of farmers posing stiffly beside their buffaloes, of smiling women, frozen over their wares in the market place; they climbed mountains and admired views. The way of life in the remote hill tribe villages scattered across the mountains was of particular interest, their colourful costumes, opium pipes and strong marijuana. Mother Pensri couldn't see the attraction. There was no electricity in many of the mountain villages and she knew for a fact there was no sanitation. But it didn't put off the *farangs*. They bought homemade knick-knacks from the Lesu people to take back home; cheap cotton wristbands, pom-pom hats and shoulder bags. One old man had so fallen in love with the simple lifestyle that he had married a young Lesu girl. A great deal of money had exchanged hands, Mother Pensri heard.

Once, on the bus coming back home, she had sat next to a young *farang*. He had struggled onto the crowded bus with a huge rucksack. The driver had made it clear the rucksack should go on top of the bus with the rest of the luggage but the young man was resolute in his refusal. He sat squeezed in next to Mother Pensri, his knees pressed miserably against the seat in front, hugging the rucksack on his lap during the entire three and a half hour journey. Mother Pensri had watched him out of the corner of her eye, wrinkling her fat little nose. He was red and hairy. His arms were especially hairy, and freckled too, which was doubly unfortunate.

Halfway into the journey she had caught his eye and smiled, nodding her head, giggling, racking her brain for the few English words she had learnt at school. *Where you go?* The young man had answered with a long sentence. At least his mouth matches the words, she had thought, nodding. He had reached into his rucksack, pulling out a dog-eared book, which he opened at a page featuring a map of north Thailand. The young man had pointed at a dot on the map and Mother Pensri had nodded again, pointing at the road winding upwards in front of them, at her chest, then back at the dot on the map. He repeated her gestures and they had both smiled. She had offered him some fried banana, urging him to eat the whole bag. They had looked through the book together, at the pictures of markets, tropical fish, southern sunsets, temples, traditional costumes, festivals, mountain mists, pretty girls and old men with wrinkled faces, peering humorously at the camera. She tried to teach him a few Thai words, pointing at the pictures, laughing at his mispronunciations. Mother Pensri especially liked the pictures of Bangkok. She had never been as far as the great city but had a beautiful picture of the glittering tiled roofs and golden spires of the Grand Palace on her wall at home. She had saved it from an old calendar.

II

A few days later she had seen the young man in the market place, sitting with a group of *farangs* at Aunty Wassana's noodle soup stall, and she had gone over to chat to Aunty Wassana, smiling and waving at the man.

'So, even *farangs* can eat your noodle soup then, Wassana.'

'You wouldn't believe it, Mother Pensri! Since the police chief opened his guest-house up by the river, I've been busier than ever. I've been up all night making pots of stock. The only problem with the *farangs* is they sit for hours on the stools after their soup is finished. Some of my regulars have to take their soup home and eat it there.'

Trust her to complain, thought Mother Pensri, determined not to give the new gold bracelet on Aunty Wassana's wrist a second glance.

'Still selling lottery tickets, Mother Pensri?'

'Oh, you know, when I've got time.' Mother Pensri fumbled in her pocket for her notebook. 'Any numbers for next week, Wassana? Looks like you might be in the middle of a lucky streak right now.'

'Oh, I've no time for *gambling* these days, Mother Pensri. I've got a business to run.'

Mother Pensri turned away, bristling. What was wrong with selling lottery tickets? Anyway, whom did Wassana think she was kidding? Mother Pensri had seen her at the funeral last month, sitting with all the other poker players. No time for gambling indeed!

Didn't Wassana know Mother Pensri had to earn a living somehow? What else was she supposed to do? Mother Pensri pursed her lips. If only her job in the fruit processing factory had worked out. But when she had gone away to work in the city with her daughter and the other village women her husband had done nothing but drink, making his ulcer worse.

The poor man was so bad he started having terrible nightmares about ghosts.

'Mother Pensri. Mother Pensri.'

It was the schoolmaster, hurrying over to where she stood at one of the vegetable stalls, staring angrily at the aubergines.

'Yes, schoolmaster? Are you after a lottery ticket?'

'No, no, nothing like that. I wanted to ask you a question.'

'A question? About what?'

'Well, I heard from the district officer's wife you have a very rare old Shan sword in your house. Is that true?'

'Yes. It belonged to my husband's great grandfather. Would you like to see it?' Mother Pensri looked up at him, shielding her eyes from the hot afternoon sun. 'Are you preparing a lesson about swords, schoolmaster?'

'No, not exactly. But I have a visitor—a foreign visitor—who would be most interested in seeing the sword.'

'A *farang*?'

The schoolmaster cleared his throat, preferring not to use the vaguely insulting word, yet anxious not to offend Mother Pensri.

'Yes, a ... *farang*. An anthropologist.'

'A what-ologist?'

'An *anthrop*ologist, Mother Pensri', repeated the schoolmaster in the tone of voice he found worked best with his pupils. 'An *an-thro-pol-o-gist*.'

III

And that was how, in the evening of the very next day, Mother Pensri found herself at home, waiting nervously for the anthropologist and the schoolmaster. Entertaining a *farang* inside her house was quite another prospect from sitting next to one on the bus. She had been awake all night worrying about what to offer her guest. Fruit? Watermelon or pineapple? Maybe some green papaya salad? Or something cooked? Did the occasion merit some *gaeng hang ley*? But would the anthropologist like chilli? Be able to eat rice? Didn't they only eat potatoes and bread? But hadn't she seen some of them enjoying Aunty Wassana's soup? Mother Pensri swept the floor one last time. She wondered if the schoolmaster would bring the anthropologist along past the market place, in front of Aunty Wassana's noodle stall. She thought with satisfaction of the expression on Wassana's face as she watched the schoolmaster lead the foreigner up the steps of Mother Pensri's house. But where had her husband disappeared to? Was he at the forbidden whisky stall? She hadn't told him about the visit. Was that them now, coming along the road? It must be! Mother Pensri hid the broom and looked in the mirror one last time, smoothing back her hair, examining her teeth for specks of food, grinning sideways at her reflection.

It amazed Mother Pensri, as she invited her guests inside: the *farang* was a woman. And fifty-one, the same age as she. It was one of the first questions she asked the schoolmaster to translate. Imagine—the same age! Mother Pensri would never have guessed. The woman was unusually thin for a *farang* and tall, with pointed elbows and a sharp nose. She wore her hair very short and made no attempt to cover the grey. In fact, she looked a bit like a man. She had small square glasses that rested halfway down her long nose, and two deep furrows ran across her big forehead. Too much thinking wasn't good for you. The skin on the woman's neck and hands was loose, lined, freckled. And she wasn't so white. Quite sunburnt actually. Her nose was peeling. Didn't she wear a hat when she went out in the sun? And no jewellery except for a tiny silver cross on a chain around her neck. She must be a Christian. Like they all were. The first *farang* Mother Pensri had ever seen was a Christian missionary. She was a little girl then and had gathered with her friends to stare at him and his big black bag full of bibles. He had disappeared into the mountains to stay in a hill tribe village. It had taken him years to convert them.

The anthropologist's bag was full of cameras and lenses, tripods, books. Mother Pensri smoothed back her hair again and whispered to the schoolmaster to ask the woman how many children she had, glancing over at the photograph of her own daughter. Pity she wasn't here. She had been clever at English. Would know what to say. What? No children? No husband either? Mother Pensri clicked her tongue against her teeth and felt sorry for the woman. Who would look after her when she was old?

'Our visitor,' said the schoolmaster, anxious not to waste any more time, 'is carrying out a field study of old Burmese and Shan swords and daggers.'

'Oh, you won't find many old swords in the fields,' answered Mother Pensri blithely. 'Most of them are kept indoors these days, schoolmaster!'

'Ahem. Quite, Mother Pensri. What I meant was that this lady is *collecting information* about swords. For a big *museum*. A big museum in *London*.'

'I see,' said Mother Pensri, smiling brightly and nodding. 'How lovely.'

'So it would be useful, Mother Pensri, if we could *see* the sword.'

'Of course, schoolmaster. I'll just go and fetch it.'

Uncle Nun kept the sword in the glass-fronted cabinet with all the other family treasures: Mother Pensri's wedding silk, the Burmese lacquerware box, her grandfather's Pali manuscripts, some faded photographs, a pile of magazines, and her daughter's old teddy bears, frayed noses pressed against the glass. Mother Pensri padded over to the cabinet, unlocking the door with a tiny key she always wore around her neck. The sword lay on the bottom shelf, wrapped in newspaper. She lifted it out carefully and brought it over, laying it in front of her two guests. To be honest, Mother Pensri didn't care for the sword. Uncle Nun's father had passed it down to him as part of the dowry, which had included a buffalo, a gold necklace with a ruby pendant and two thousand baht—quite a lot of money in those days. The buffalo had been sold a long time since and Mother Pensri planned to give the necklace to her daughter on her wedding day. With any luck, her daughter would find a good man, a man she truly loved. But the sword, rare and beautiful, left Mother Pensri cold. It reminded her of the wedding night, of her mother's fluttering hands and her father's grimly determined face, of a younger Nun dancing in front of their guests in a drunken imitation of a ceremonial sword dance, a distant memory she tried to shake off as she watched the schoolmaster unwrap the newspaper. The anthropologist picked up and admired the scabbard, its silver chape, pulling the sword out, running her fingers across the decorative hilt and along the thick, still sharp blade. Mother Pensri shuddered and went into the kitchen to fetch a tray piled with fruit, sticky coconut sweets and a pot of steaming jasmine tea.

As she poured the tea the schoolmaster and the anthropologist were deep in conversation. A glossy book lay open at a page with pictures of similar swords. Mother Pensri pushed the plate of coconut sweets in the direction of the woman, smiling and nodding with raised eyebrows to encourage the woman to taste the sweets, which had taken her several hours to make.

'The anthropologist would like to know,' said the schoolmaster, helping himself to the sweets, 'how old the sword is.'

'Heavens, schoolmaster. Uncle Nun's great-grandfather ...' Mother Pensri calculated rapidly, an expert with numbers. 'Maybe one hundred and fifty years?'

The schoolmaster and the anthropologist talked together in low, excited voices, flicking though the pages of the book and examining the sword's hilt with a magnifying glass. The anthropologist still hadn't touched her tea or tasted the sweets.

'This sword,' said the schoolmaster at last, brushing flakes of coconut from his shirt front, 'is most valuable, Mother Pensri. It dates back to the nineteenth century wars between the Shans and the northern Thais. It's a near-perfect example of its kind. A rarity. A one-off. An *antique*. Think of it, Mother Pensri: your forefathers probably used this very sword in battle, defending the village.' He leaned over her, his voice low. 'It might even have been used to fight off the foreign invaders, to keep the colonialists at bay. The only country in the region not to be colonised, just think about that.' He leant back again and folded his arms triumphantly. 'Have you any idea, Mother Pensri, just *how* valuable this is?'

Mother Pensri gazed at the sword with a new respect. What was the schoolmaster suggesting? Was the sword worth a lot of money? Mother Pensri cleared her throat.

'Of course. Of course I know it's valuable. It's an antique. One hundred and fifty years old, at least. Maybe older.' Mother Pensri could feel the eyes of the anthropologist and the schoolmaster upon her. 'My husband Uncle Nun,' she concluded lamely, 'is a fine sword dancer, you know. He never misses an opportunity to dance with the sword.'

The schoolmaster and the anthropologist leaned together and conferred for several minutes. The anthropologist produced a calculator from the bag. The schoolmaster shook his head and the anthropologist shrugged, glancing up at Mother Pensri.

'Mother Pensri,' he began, the tips of his long fingers placed together in a pyramid, 'the anthropologist is interested in your sword. So interested, in fact, that she is willing to *buy* it, take it back to London and hang it up in the museum. To give it pride of place in an exhibition. For *posterity*.'

Mother Pensri stared at the schoolmaster, the tips of his fingers, her mind racing. Posterity? How much would *that* cost? And what would Nun say?

'How much?'

'Twenty thousand baht, Mother Pensri.'

Mother Pensri patted her hair and looked through the doorway, outside the house, to where dusk was falling on the village. Men and children were making their way home to shower, to rest after work and school, to eat. She didn't have much time. Bare feet sounded on the steps up to the house; Mother Pensri felt the familiar sinking of her heart. But instead of the husband she expected, Sergeant Yud appeared in the doorway, breathing heavily, weaving slightly, bemused at the scene before him. Tripping over the tray and upsetting the coconut sweets, he sank, a circus elephant, to his knees, and brought his palms together in front of his nose, bowing elaborately first to the schoolmaster and then to the *farang*. His sense of propriety satisfied, he wobbled back on his heels, turning to Mother Pensri with raised hands.

'Moth'r Pensri,' he slurred, 'your husband's at th'whisky stall. Sleepin'. Fell off th'stool.' Sergeant Yud giggled. 'Cel'brations.' He jabbed his thumb proudly at his fat chest, grinning around the room. 'Won at th'cock fight.'

'Fine, I'll be along to fetch him home soon. Thank you, Sergeant Yud,' said Mother Pensri, getting up, her arms outstretched, shooing the policeman's bulk away from her guests. Sergeant Yud backed obediently out of the room on all fours, turning at the door to negotiate the steps.

Mother Pensri waited until he'd gone, cleared her throat and held her head high.

'Thirty thousand.'

The schoolmaster turned to the anthropologist, whispering.

'Twenty-five,' he said at last.

'Twenty-eight,' said Mother Pensri, ignoring the schoolmaster, holding up eight fingers to the anthropologist. The thin woman nodded, smiling over the tops of her glasses at Mother Pensri, as though the two women had known one another a long, long time.

IV

'Well, Mother Pensri, I see you had some important guests last night?' Aunty Wassana said.

'Important guests? I suppose you could say that, yes. The schoolmaster brought a *farang* to look at Uncle Nun's old Shan sword. She took ever so many photographs. For an exhibition.' Mother Pensri cleared her throat. 'In a *museum*. In *London*.'

Mother Pensri didn't give Aunty Wassana time for any more questions, moving past the noodle stall quickly. The sale of the sword was her business. The transaction had been swift; tissue paper was produced from the anthropologist's bag to wrap up the sword and the money had been passed over before she could even think to change her mind. After the schoolmaster and the *farang* had left Mother Pensri had rolled the money up into a tight bundle and had hidden it amongst her underwear. Then, before going to the whisky stall to collect Uncle

Nun, she had gone into the backyard with his long knife and chopped down a length of bamboo. She had wrapped the bamboo up in the old newspaper, laying it back in the wooden cabinet, next to the faded wedding pictures. Her dowry. It would be months before he found out. The schoolmaster wouldn't say anything; she had his word. He wouldn't want Uncle Nun on his tail anyway. And Nun wouldn't look for it until the End of Lent celebrations. No more ceremonial sword dances, she thought victoriously.

Mother Pensri hurried into the market place. Dawn was often the best time to catch the vendors. The night before, some of them might have had dreams that could be interpreted as particular numbers to buy in next week's underground lottery. The early morning bus back to the city was just leaving, pulling out on to the road from the bus station beside the market. Everyone glanced up to see who was on the bus, as everyone always did. Mother Pensri saw the anthropologist, squashed against the window, her soft bag set doggedly on her knees, glasses pushed up on top of her grey hair. She looked younger without her glasses. She was brave to be travelling alone in a foreign country with no man to protect her, Mother Pensri thought. All that money on her too: anything could happen. The *farang* smiled, waving at Mother Pensri as the driver changed gears and the bus trundled along the village main street, gathering speed.

ANDREA MCNICOLL was born in the west of Scotland. Tired of the endless drizzle, she escaped to live in Thailand for 12 years, running a restaurant and working as a translator. *Fat of the Land* is her first novel, which was written with the support of a Scottish Arts Council bursary. A recent graduate of the Glasgow University Creative Writing MPhil, Andrea is now working on a second book, a multi-protagonist novel set in the northern Thai city of Chiang Mai.

Missing Breath

Chee Lay Tan

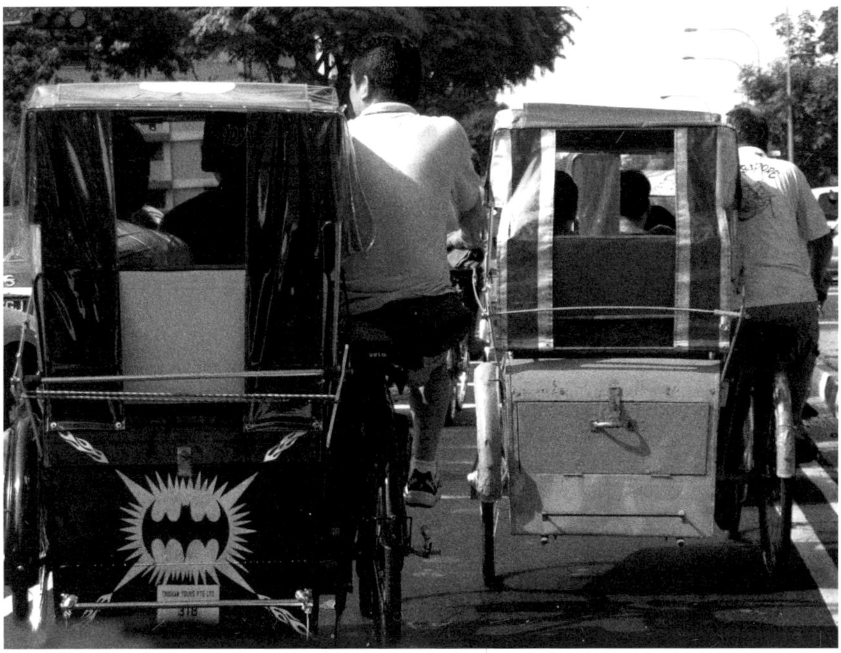

Born in Singapore, Chee Lay Tan has studied and lived in Singapore, Taiwan and in the United Kingdom. He is a keen photographer and poet, and is currently enrolled in a PhD at the University of Cambridge, working on his dissertation on exiled Chinese poets. He was awarded the Singapore Young Artist Award in 2004 and the Singapore Youth Award (Arts and Culture) in 2006. His previous literary publications are all in Chinese; 'Missing Breath' is his first English poem in print.

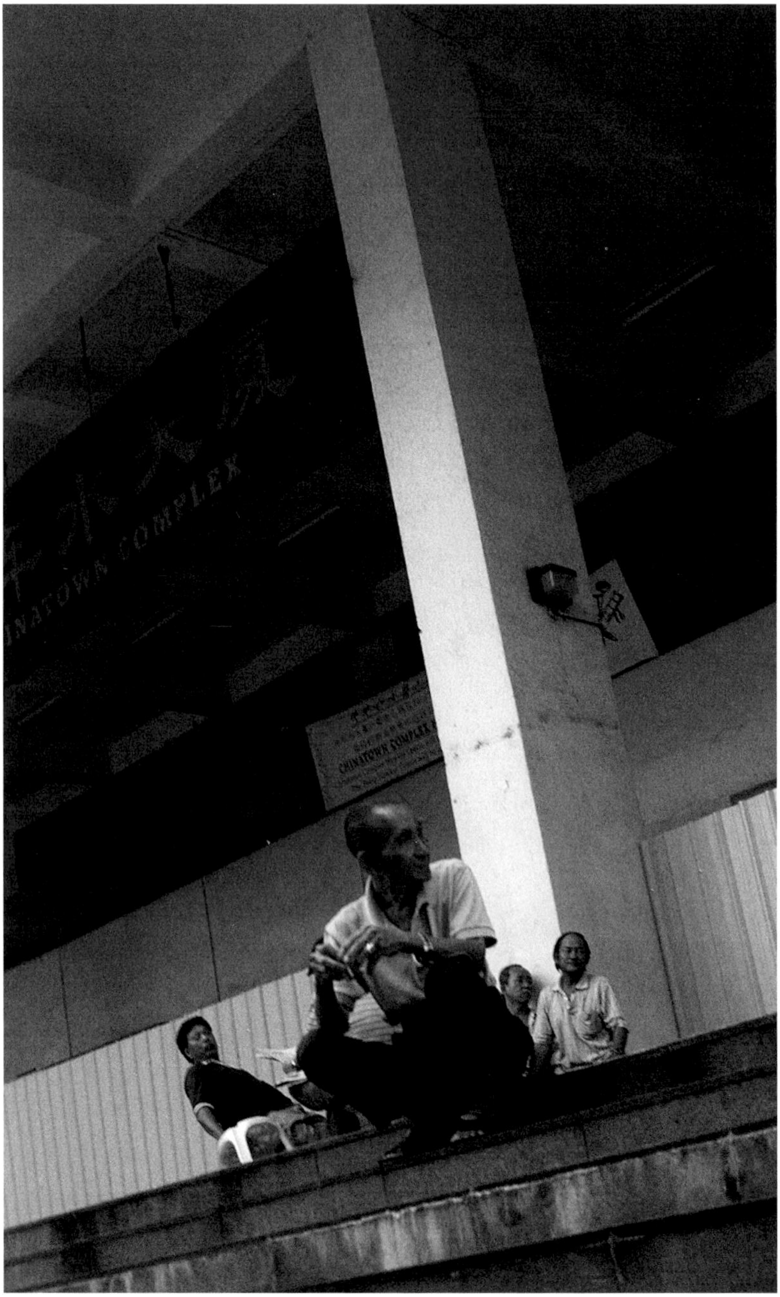
CHINATOWN COMPLEX

Missing Breath
(in Tiananmen Square)

a loudhailer is missing in the empty
square
the boots have marched
the wings have flown,
an ant
has lost its way home.

without wind, flags are deep
in meditation,
in a square where even the bricks
remain suspicious.

the voices
must have left with
the loudhailer,
now I can only wait
for tomorrow's single breath
to shout
yesterday's forgotten command.

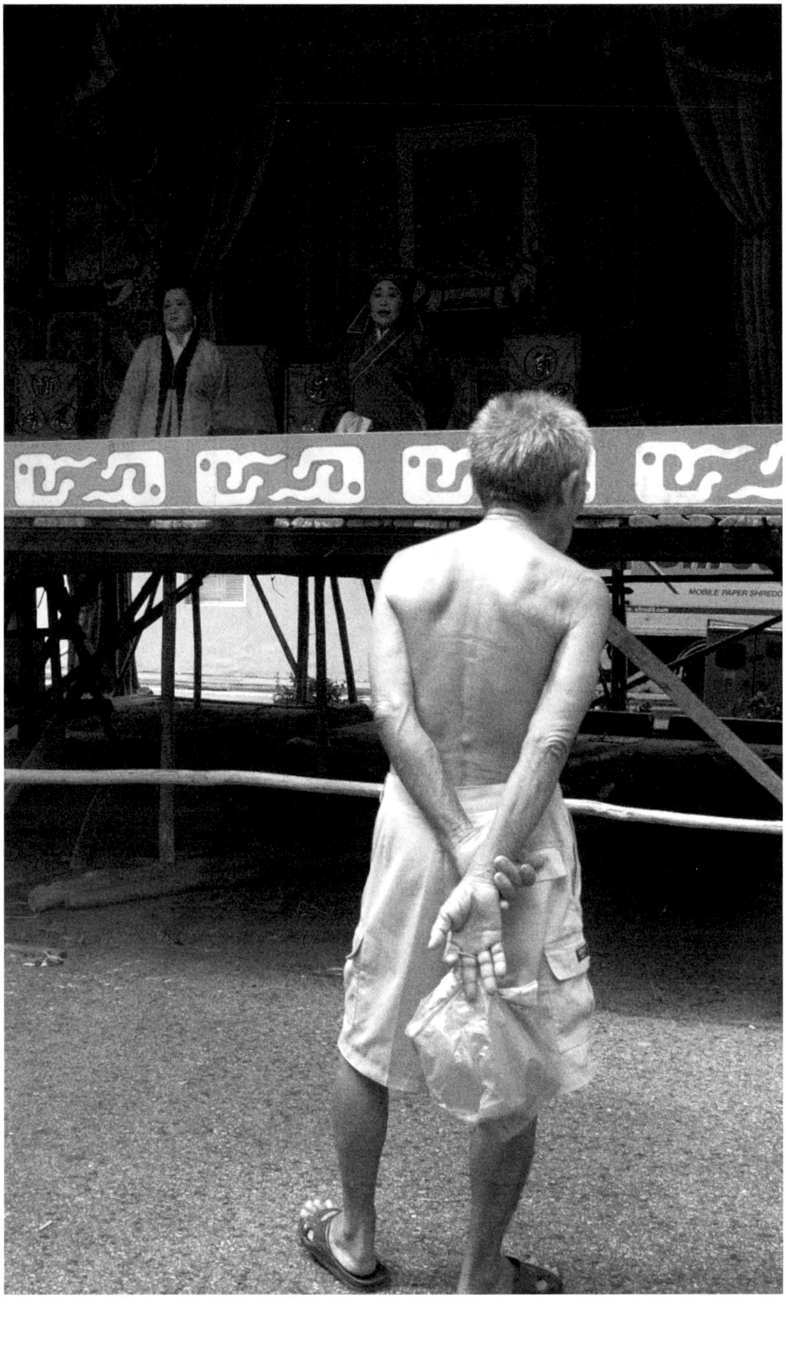

TRANSLATING PHAM THI HOAI
THE INVISIBILITY OF THE TRANSLATOR

TON THAT QUYNH DU

Maintaining the invisibility of the translator while making the process of translation more visible is a paradox. Is it achievable, and what really is the responsibility of the translator?

The general belief is that translators ought to be invisible on the page. Such assertions encourage the view that the work of the translator is routine and automatic, that translations are similar to photographic reproductions of paintings, mechanical in process, unthinkingly faithful but lacking in creative spirit. Such assertions fly in the face of the nature of translation as I experience it.

Most of my known translating has been for one author, Pham Thi Hoai, from Vietnamese into my adopted language, English. I have translated her debut novel, *Crystal Messenger*, and a collection of short stories, *Sunday Menu*, published in 2006.

If translating Hoai's work means bringing the English reader into the world of her fiction, giving the English reader an experience similar to that enjoyed by her Vietnamese readers, then translating Hoai's work demands close engagement by the translator with the text at all levels, in ways that are intimate and at times interpretive.

Apart from mediating between two languages and two literary traditions with very different sets of conventions and artistic vocabularies, the translator also mediates on another level: that of selector, not only of words and whole phrases, but also, as in short fiction collections, whole stories—choosing which stories to include and which to leave out. In a way, putting together a collection of short stories is a bit like composing a literary portrait of the writer. The translator is faced with choosing those pieces that best capture the essence of the writer's work. And the translator's choice is influenced by how he or she sees the author's work, how it is understood and how it is crafted. For example, in the collection *Sunday Menu* I did not include two important polemic works by Hoai, *The Poets' Republic* and *The Government Inspector Visits*, primarily because we were more interested in a portrait of Hoai the writer than Hoai the intellectual dissident.

And how do I see Hoai's work? What is the essence of Hoai's fiction that really needs to come across as a defining conceit of this writer's work? Two years ago, I was fishing off the rocks in Lunawanna, an isolated spot in Bruny Island, on a perfect Tasmanian day. The sea sparkled, the breeze blew gently, the waves lapped over the rocks, and it dawned on me then that nature was completely absent from the world of Hoai's fiction.

Not for her the struggle of man against nature, *Old Man and The Sea,* nor seeking solitude in the mountain to contemplate the insignificance of mankind, but instead, the world of her fiction is packed with busy humans living in close friction with each other. There is a relentless focus on the biological needs of her characters. In *Crystal Messenger* the narrator's family of six live in one room, queuing up daily to share a single public water tap with nine hundred other people. In *Sunday Menu* poor cyclo drivers flock to have a cheap meal at a street-side eatery.

In this tight and uncomfortable world, romantic love is largely absent; it afflicts only the few unfortunate ones, usually the incurable romantics and the gullible, as the narrator in 'Universal Love' observes of her mother's taste for men:

> [M]other continued to open her heart to everyone, to the men whose desires refused to mature with their increasing age, men who were lost among their own herds, men whose sole aim in life was to revenge the undeserved success of others, men shorter than one-metre-sixty, men with broken hearts, men who checked small change given back by paperboys, men who exaggerated their social connections, men who could not find a

> way to divorce their wives, men who naively rushed headlong into syphilis, men who energetically tried to absorb and disseminate the latest unique ideas, men who desperately resisted the tragedy of being forgotten, and her top priority was reserved for the gloomy.

Love is not happening, however, to the narrator in 'Second-hand', a cynical battle-hardened street trader selling second-hand clothes, a rough character being pursued by an even rougher diamond. Here is how she sees him:

> It also disgusts me to see you sit there, yawning till your eyes water, picking your nose and examining the blob of snot on your greying index finger before squishing it on the table. Do feel free to sit there and entertain yourself by cleaning your orifices. Fifteen minutes per orifice; at this rate you will soon be a clean man, but I can't quite stand the disgusting way you go about it.

Yet, at the end of 'Second-hand' she accepts his proposal for marriage.

It's not surprising that death, the biological end of living things, features prominently in the world of Hoai's fiction. There is a symbolic death in 'The Toll of the Sea', a violent death in bizarre circumstances in 'Saigon Tailor', and in my view the death scene in 'Sunday Menu' is most instructive.

'Sunday Menu' is set in a kerbside eatery serving the cheapest food to cyclo drivers—the poorest workers of Hanoi. It's run by the narrator's mother, who keeps costs down by all possible means:

> I knew for a fact that today's soup was yesterday's soup disguised by freshly chopped shallots, and yesterday's was really that of the day before; that inside that pot over there, happily simmering away and gently browning to a mahogany colour, were the 2.1 kilos of rotten, flyblown meat bought at the market at the end of the day—flies and their egg sacks dotted that piece of meat like black beans and sesame seeds.

Meanwhile, the narrator's grandma lies by herself in an attic room, waiting for death to come, dreaming of the culinary delights of her former aristocratic days. Every Sunday the narrator visits her grandma. To keep grandma happily cocooned in her nostalgic dreams, she makes a false report, telling grandma about the glorious food being cooked at home, using the names of dishes she reads in cookbooks at the local library. Many things happen, then grandma dies, but our narrator leaves grandma's body in the room and continues to visit every day, bringing with her a plate of real food for the deceased, a funeral banquet. Here is the description of her last visit:

> The incense smoke curled thick and the flies swarmed black. [...] I couldn't see her clearly, she seemed a little more grandly bloated, bursting at the seams of her clothes, destined to disintegrate tomorrow, to be taken away by flies and ants on a trip back to Mother Earth. She seemed to lean towards the colour of Buddha, with her white chiffon blouse having gone almost brown. A purple flower seemed to have blossomed on her smile.
>
> [...] Grandma was lying on the floor. Her face was turned towards the door waiting for me, her mouth next to a bowl of shark-fin soup. A terrible flow of slime oozed from her mouth to the bowl, or was it rising from the bowl to her mouth? I couldn't tell. I tried not to panic, asking her to return to her old place, to turn around to watch the clouds floating past Grandpa, it's better that way, lying down like this is no way to enjoy a banquet. But the two wobbly timber planks had collapsed upon her possessions. The feather-light goddesses of her fine china chamberpot lay shattered. I closed my eyes tight. When I opened them again I saw millions of busy maggots.

'Busy maggots' is an odd but accurate observation. We usually think of maggots as revolting, disgusting, not as busy beings. But if we take time to reflect on it, all that they do is go about their own lives searching for nutrients to sustain themselves, just like the cyclo drivers feasting themselves at the eatery, or indeed any of the six billion busy humans in the world.

In terms of style, I have come to appreciate Hoai's dry wit and the way she combines it with insightful observations to give sketches that sum up the essence of her characters in only a few lines. But there are also other occasions when her keen eye for detail provides comprehensive descriptions, missing nothing. An example of the first is found in 'Saigon Tailor' at a dressmaking class. It is set in post-war Vietnam and deals with young women from the countryside who come to the capital city Hanoi in search of a better life:

> I felt that it was the right time to sew him a pair of shorts so I took the material upstairs to ask Tuc to cut it for me. Just plain material and I counted on the improvising touch of the artistic teacher, Tuc. But Tuc wasn't there, only Quyet lying on the table right underneath the overhead fan, tapping his gut while singing *La Dieu Bong*. A few strands of his hair were swimming in a bowl of vegetable soup served on a tray placed on the table next to his head. He asked me what I wanted to make. I said a pair of shorts. He said, 'Follow the basic cut for a pair of pants, just cut off the legs.' I thought that it wouldn't be quite right, that this special present needed the improvising artistic touch of Teacher Tuc, so I tried to take leave, excusing myself by saying it was his lunch break. But he got up and said, 'Give it to me,' and two seconds later the material had been cut and he returned to his lying position, his hair again swimming in the bowl of soup.

As a contrast, in 'Vision Impaired' we are offered an absorbing and detailed description through the ears of the narrator receiving a massage from a masseuse that has been brought home by her husband.

> For the duration of the session, the master took his time, leisurely explaining to my husband every move and every trick. 'This is punching, fluid and shallow punches only, withdraw as soon as the blows connect, the force coming from the wrist and not the arm. A good pummelling must sing cracking pleasure to the ears. I've said *tam quat* is for the common folk. Our folk like noisy crowds. That's why we fear solitary confinement more than execution. At executions, at least there's gunfire and yelling spectators. This is called patting, your hand forming the dome shape of the tortoise's shell, cupping air and slapping down. You must also make a nice slapping sound. [...] This is called catching the mouse. Along

> the back, here and here, under each side of the ridge, there hides a mouse, you have to flush it out to make it run like this. This is called the march of a thousand ants. Use the tips of your fingers lightly, but the customer must feel the goose-pimples rising if you're any good at it. [...] Now this is called the wading stork: your fingers walk like the deliberate and rhythmic feet of a stork. Take your time and don't rush. You can also call it the pecking stork, pecking in single strokes, in a leisurely and unhurried manner. A flurry of typist finger strokes may cause the customer to feel he's reaching the height of pleasure, but that'll be no good. The height of pleasure must be when it hurts the most, the waves of pain followed by a moment of feeling faint and then, a few seconds later, pleasure hits at its most extreme. [...] And now, the height of pleasure, it's simply called plucking. You start plucking here at this spot of the back, and move down, all the way to the coccyx, like this.'

Although imageries can be culturally bound and need sensitive treatment, bringing them across into another language can be attained with reasonable attention and moderate competence on the part of the translator. More interesting and more challenging is when language itself is central to the enjoyment of the story. Let's again look at 'Saigon Tailor'.

'Saigon Tailor' begins with the line, 'Saigon Tailor is not in Saigon, not in Cali', taking the reader to a dressmaking shop named Saigon Tailor, but it's not in Saigon, not in California, but in Ha Noi, the seat of revolutionary power that prevailed over the Sai Gon regime. It's a succinct introduction to the post-war economic reforms of Vietnam, when fashion replaced firearms, and a cheeky comment on Ha Noi's cultural cringe: revolutionaries are not known for their confidence and good taste in the fashion stakes.

But there is also musicality in the opening sentence. Hoai once told me that the titles of her stories serve as time signatures, and that the opening sentences are the conductor's baton that sets the pace, rhythm and the musical tone for the rest of the story. *Tiem May Sai Gon khong o sai gon khong o cali.* Those rythmic opening sixteen syllables tune the reader's inner ear for the language that follows, a very specific language of the street traders of Hanoi.

I was lucky that I had experienced this street trader language first-hand before I translated 'Saigon Tailor'. In 1999 my family and I lived in Vietnam for nearly four months, courtesy of an Asialink residency, and while in Hanoi I used to go to the market everyday to buy food. One day I went very early to avoid the crowds. Nobody was around except for a group of female small traders circling around watching two women involved in a particularly nasty argument. One was obviously having the upper-hand, delivering abuse after abuse at her hapless victim who was unable to answer back simply because the abuses came thick and fast, witty and cruelly funny, one abuse gliding rhythmically into the next without a break, with the unstoppable momentum of a T-54 tank. At one point, the dominating woman actually dropped her pants and demonstrated what she might do to her victim's husband, complete with thrusting movements in rhythm with her abuses. Although abusive and aggressive, her language was also creative and extremely powerful. The owner of Saigon Tailor, Tuyet, speaks in a way that reminds me of this street language. Here is an example of Tuyet's language when the narrator found her in a raging mood:

> As I came down the stairs, the girls were trying to calm Tuyet down, holding her at the waist as if trying to keep her guts from spilling out. They might well have been able to hold her guts but nobody could ever hold back her tongue. [...] I came down the stairs straight into the middle of her sentence, '... making a mess and not tidying up after yourself finishing with the iron and not unplugging it is just like going to the toilet and not flushing like shitting and not shovelling it away leaving this old woman to clean up after you, you little young sluts so that you can sit and chat among yourselves don't say that you've come here to learn not one of you can manage to sew a straight line your buttons are uneven like the dirt tracks of your paddy fields your buttonholes are as coarse and hairy as your cunts don't bother calling yourself students I'll send you all packing this is a place for serious learning we are all educated and cultured here this is not a bloody brothel this is not a market that you can come and go as you bloody please in this day and age nobody cares about anybody if I don't look after you who would ...'

George Steiner once said, 'The translator invades, extracts, and brings home.' Having brought home the language, the translator then has to find some way of placing it. Where in contemporary Australian usage of English do I place the sort of language found in 'Saigon Tailor'? I have an adequate knowledge of Australian abusive language, but I don't know if there is anything quite its equivalent. If there isn't an obvious equivalent sub-register in the target language to aim for, somehow the translator has to imagine that there is one and go for it.

The translator has to sense what works and what doesn't, what sounds right and what sounds wrong. What guides the translator is his or her own appreciation of the original text and an ability to render it in another language, both of which are affected by the translator's own life experiences.

So, what do I make of the question of the (in)visibility of the translator. I am tempted to quote the Hanoi-based translator Duong Tuong and say that a good translation should have a hundred percent of the author and a hundred percent of the translator. But this observation somehow doesn't quite capture the sense of close engagement between the translator, the author and the original text. Perhaps I should borrow the words, used in a very different context, of the critic Nguyen Hung Quoc, and say that a good translation is the 'love child of a three-way relationship' between the translator, the author and the original text.

The translator may prefer not to be in the limelight, and his or her presence is not always conspicuous. But the translator is there, definitely there.

TON THAT QUYNH DU was born and grew up in the old imperial city of Hue, Vietnam. In 1972 he received a Colombo Plan scholarship and came to study in Australia. He has worked as a translator and court interpreter, and has taught at Deakin University, Monash University and the Australian National University. In 2000 his translation of Pham Thi Hoai's novel, *Crystal Messenger,* won the Victorian Premier's Award in the literary translation category. His translation of *Sunday Menu*, a collection of short stories by Pham Thi Hoai, was published by Pandanus Books in 2006.

VISION IMPAIRED

PHAM THI HOAI

On the first session I put on three layers of clothes above and two layers below the waist. My husband said this *tam quat* master wasn't a master of martial arts with wall-piercing fingers, so there was no need to protect myself with so much armour. The master was wearing dark glasses, my husband added, and wouldn't be able to tell a woman from a man, if he hadn't been told. But I thought otherwise, that clothes were not just to shield or to conceal your body; even in coffins, bodies are fully clothed. I wanted to be tactful to show my goodwill the first time a stranger's hands were to touch my body. Not all men are as progressive as my husband, and the blind men that I know all seem to be behind the times, as if they live in a faraway world of their own, a world where the sun neither rises nor sets. I was fearful that if I was not careful I might cause offence to a person with a disability. Feeling the bra beneath the thick layers of my full set of clothes, surely he would understand that I regarded him as a person of goodwill. Then both of us could trust each other more easily, as not only was this my first time, he had never worked on a woman before.

Tam quat is not for women. My husband had to go through a great deal of trouble to bring the master home. What kind of a world are we living in, my husband complained, that it's easier to hire someone to beat up your wife than to find someone to give her a thumping back rub? Everywhere he went, they all thought he was making mischief and found polite excuses to turn him down. Women bring bad luck, they would say. Only this master answered my husband in full. 'Wouldn't it be better for you to buy your wife some of those machines? Machines that massage, vibrate, suck and slap, machines that work on your feet, massage your belly, tickle your armpits, that use infrared technology. Everything under the sun is available these days. Those Chinese machines with plastic nibs and sticks that rub and beat you simultaneously, they are a penny a dozen and they last you a lifetime. I don't know why you bother with us, we who have nothing but our humble bare hands. We aren't worth your trouble.'

My husband liked the mocking acerbic tone of this master. When he persisted in asking, the master gave him a further blast: 'And if you're after a genuine experience then take your wife to a hotel. There real people give you real services. A massage to freshen your skin on your way in, a sauna to warm your flesh on your way out. It's entertaining, gentle and elegant. All we can do here is twist your neck and crack your back, quite savage and beastly really, not at all suitable for women.'

My husband became even more interested. He has a natural affinity with the eccentric. He would befriend anyone with a reputation of being a nonconformist, sparing no effort to entertain them at home. For a long time our house was full of artistic guests, but after a while he came to the conclusion that they were just pretending to be eccentric, because if one harbours the wish to be celebrated by others then one cannot disdain society from a distance. In any case, these artists proved to be thorny and unique only in pure talk, their artistic creations as smooth and conformist as the next, their sense of abrasive individualism nowhere to be seen. In the end my husband didn't quite know what to do with them. For a while he regretted the missed chance to make friends with a famous non-artist, a former official of the French time, who claimed to follow what he called thank-you excuse-me ism, who declared himself the last person in the world who still knew how to use these two endangered phrases; as long as he was alive, those were the only words he ever uttered. But unfortunately my husband came a little too late. The man's tongue had frozen stiff and my husband got there just in time to take his body to Van Dien cemetery for burial.

So for the whole of this year, my husband has been feeling sorry for himself and for the rest of mankind. To him, the young have lots of front but not much flair, the old are out of touch but not out of the ordinary. This *tam quat* master, although young, spoke with the maturity and depth of an independent thinker who held his own considered opinions. My husband turned on all his charm, taking the master out to have a few drinks of sparkling wine at a place where the owner had a reputation for being arrogant, serving only a select few. In the end, the master accepted my husband's request out of a sense of obligation, but added that he had never worked on a woman before, so if something went wrong he would count on our magnanimity.

At first, my husband told me to lie down on a divan to be within easy reach of the master. But the master said, 'We're more used to sitting down on a mat. I hear that at the Institute of Traditional Medicine they offer a training course for masseurs where the patients lie on a table and the practitioners stand up, dressed in white blouses. But *tam quat* is a tradition of the common people. Let's remain informal, it suits our style better.'

My husband quickly rolled out a mat, saying that he was in total agreement with the master; this this was an intimate space, not a public arena, and that we were here to enjoy ourselves in comfort, not to endure stiff formality, and that the the master should also feel at ease here. The master sat down on the mat. I climbed down from the divan and lay down. My husband said, 'Her head is to your left and her feet to your right, master.' He had tidied up our house with care, as usually our home was full of haphazardly placed furniture, books, pot plants, bric-a-brac, gifts from our onetime artistic friends and curiosities collected by my husband. This master did not have a walking stick, nor a dog or a child to guide his way, as if he expected things to get out of his way and not the other way round.

I lay down rigid. I felt restrictive no matter which position I took—on my stomach, on my side or my back—as if lying down was something I'd never done before in my life. Lying on my stomach, my buttocks felt protrusive; the more I pressed my thighs together, the more prominent the buttocks felt. But if I relaxed my thighs it felt a little revealing. Lying on my side showed even more. On my back, it felt wide open. As soon as the master's hands touched me, my body tensed up, a mass of watchful hypersensitive flesh.

The master said, 'Your wife's not comfortable.' My husband asked, 'How come my wife is not comfortable? What do you mean, not comfortable?' The master replied, 'When we were young, on the occasions when we got a caning, we usually tensed up like this.' My husband laughed out loud, gave a long commentary on love delivered through the cane, and said, 'That's why

I love this form of traditional massage. It's physical and unrestrained, every blow as memorable as the next, unlike the so-called massages of modern times. I hate pretentious fakes. Give her the real experience, you must not pull your punches.'

I like whatever my husband likes and detest what he hates, from the very beginning to the very end. To be a wife is to trust your fate in someone else's hand, to give him all you've got, body and soul, holding nothing back as your own. My husband regards that attitude as too passive, taking the end point, obligation, as the starting point of the relationship. So I alter my position a little, saying that I trust him with my body and soul, that I entwine my fate with his, because we share our hearts. I don't see what difference it makes to have a common heart or a fateful obligation as a starting point. But if it pleases him, then so be it.

The master said, 'Oh yes, we like to use a bit of force too. Clients who get a real pummelling feel that they get their money's worth. Today we'll work free of charge on the hands and the feet, the marginal extremities that aren't worth charging for. If you feel that it does no harm then the next time we won't hold anything back, Mr Teacher.' My husband agreed, but stressed, 'You hold back only this first time, yes? Next time we must dispense with all these silly formalities. It wouldn't be a genuine experience of *tam quat* if we hide behind these qualifications and hedges.'

Each of my hands is less than twenty square centimetres in size but the master took a whole fifteen minutes to finish. Most exquisite was the care with which he rolled my fingers, caressing every square millimetre. After half an hour, my husband joked, 'By now you probably know my wife's hands better than I do', and the master replied, 'You've got a point there, Mr Teacher. It's quite common for people to know a face or a voice. To recognise someone by their smell is less common, and rarer still by the sounds of their footsteps. But most uncommon is to know somebody by their hands. That's not surprising for the old days when we were unaccustomed to shaking hands, but even in these modern, hand-shaking times we still don't know each other's hands. Even those who spend all day wringing their obsequious hands don't know their own hands.' My husband broke in, 'So you must really know other people's hands.' The master said, 'No, not really. We know only the backs usually. Our customers aren't concerned with hands; it's the back that's most important. All we need to do for their hands is to crack the knuckles, making ten sharp sounds, which takes ten seconds. That's all it takes to keep them happy. With some customers only nine joints crack, taking nine seconds—less than the time it takes for a perfunctory handshake, Mr Teacher.'

My husband said he'd like to hear the ten cracking sounds, just to see what it was like. The master placed one of my hands, with its palm open, inside his palm then closed in. His thumb moved smoothly along the knuckles of my hand as though they were the ivory keys of a piano. Four neat cracking sounds. Then his thumb moved quickly to the lower knuckles at the base of my fingers. Another four sounds, four notes lower than the previous, then his thumb and his index finger closed in around my thumb and neatly cupped it, making a low muffled cracking sound. The tenth note came from somewhere deep below the base of my thumb. My other hand also sang ten notes. My husband was impressed. The master said, 'It's a simple little trick really. Anyone with a little dexterity can do it. If you practice at it you'd master it in no time, Mr Teacher.'

Then it was my feet, and my husband was visibly moved. When the master massaged the mound of my foot, rubbing each toe and between the toes, massaging the ankle, then placing my foot, which also measured less than twenty centimetre squares, in the palm of one hand, the other hand covering my foot from above, gently nursing my foot in the way one would protect a fragile little bird, my husband smiled at me. I smiled back. When I am unsure what my husband might be thinking, I always smile. The master's warm hand closed around my ankle. His other hand chopped, knocked, and slapped unceasingly on the sole of my foot. He tickled me lightly and my foot jerked back in a movement that jolted from heel to knee. My husband said, 'And you said that *tam quat* was barbaric.'

'Yes,' the master said. He yanked hard and my ankle sang a low snapping note. 'Or you could say it's common, Mr Teacher', he added. Again he yanked hard and my other ankle cracked with the same low, sharp sound. My feet remained attached to my legs, yet they felt so light and so weightless, soft and lazy like two large wilting leaves, and so comfortable; all they wanted was to remain forever in this blissful state, so that they could continue to be so nursed, tickled and indulged. They'd become spoiled rotten.

'You know, modern pleasures are too easily available but ephemeral, and people with depth, like you, Mr Teacher, feel unsatisfied and turn to the simplicity of traditional practices. It doesn't take much to learn, otherwise people of darkness like us couldn't get a grasp on it. There is no foundation for it really. We simply copy from others, the whole lot, the good and the bad. We don't know what to discard or what is of real value, so we adopt everything in the hope that it might do the trick. Outsiders don't see how it works. They think it's mysterious, a bit like thinking that snakes must have legs to move so fast. Acupuncture or acupressure may have some scientific basis, but just to give a rub and a thump like this, orang-utans can do just as good a job. It's a way for us to eke out a living. We would love to have another way to make a living but as fate has dictated it to be this way, we have no choice.'

My husband didn't know what to say. We have had many eccentric visitors to our home, and sometimes they speak in profound ways that border on insanity, but no one was quite as ambiguous and difficult to pin down as this master. All day long he spoke in a mocking but humorous tone. We didn't know if he wanted to keep a distance from us or to get closer. Did he regard us with contempt or did he think highly of us? Was he being honest with us or was he testing the water with his circular style of talk? But one thing was clear: professionally, he knew what he was doing, and my husband insisted on ordering a *cyclo* to take him home and bring him back the following day. My husband did not say it out loud, but I knew this enigmatic master was to be a welcome visitor to our home for quite a while.

The second day, my husband was even more nervous than I was. He urged me to lie down on the mat before the master arrived. I lay down on my stomach, closed my eyes and let my mind roam. The master didn't know my face. His hands sometimes felt warm and sometimes refreshingly cool. He spoke with a mocking voice full of barbs. The way he talked, he was probably having fun at my husband's expense. Perhaps he was also contemptuous of me. But if that was true, then how come he caressed my feet with such loving care? Even the most dedicated and indulgent pedicurist would be no comparison. I now knew that I had two feet, not just for walking, but also for making demands, to be spoiled rotten and even for daydreaming. Our feet work so hard, yet I brush my hair several times a day and never brushed my feet. Every night my husband sought out my breasts several times but ignored my feet. But after the master's first visit, all of a sudden, he gave my feet a long and wet kiss with more passion and urgency than the kiss he gave to my lips, and it felt deliciously fresh and unfamiliar, just like our wedding night. I was moved to tears. There wouldn't be that many women who have had their toes sucked by their husband.

My husband told me to wear a silk blouse and a pair of silk pants. 'That's sufficient,' he said, 'men usually wear only a pair of shorts at *tam quat*. I didn't go through all these troubles to bring him here to massage your layers of sartorial resistance,' he added. 'This is all about your skin and flesh which I love and indulge. I am doing this for you; you would never have sought these pleasures for yourself. What's more, too much protection would suggest that we suspect the other party of ill intent. My wife is not like those girls who sit with legs crossed into knots and walk with joined knees. Too much protection is just like an invitation to invade.'

The silk made me feel soft, or maybe the master's touch had become familiar. Had I already begun to feel in tune with his hands? First came the circular movements, rubbing gently, moving from the shoulder blades along the back, spreading across the small of the back, down towards my buttocks. Again I smiled at my husband. The master said, 'The back is alright, but the shoulders and buttocks will take quite a bit of work.' My husband looked perplexed. The master explained, 'It will take only two sessions to loosen the muscles of the back, that's no problem. The shoulders and the neck are so stiff and knotted, they'll take at least a week. But the sides seem a little bit misaligned. We're not sure yet. If it's a curved spine, then there's nothing we can do, Mr. Teacher, you'll have to get a doctor. *Tam quat* masters can make no difference whatsoever.' My husband begged the master to examine his wife more closely. The master insisted that his ability was limited. While this conversation was happening, my husband's hands moved to one of my buttocks and began to massage it, and the master's hands the other one. The stiff formality of the day before was well and truly discarded, as agreed. In the end, my husband conceded to the master's wish, and praised the master's remarkable humility, so different from the boastful quacks, who were equipped with only cheap sticky medicated patches but claimed to be able to treat all kinds of illness. He also quietly congratulated himself for having a keen eye and good judgment of people.

For the duration of the session, the master took his time, leisurely explaining to my husband every move and every trick. 'This is punching, fluid and shallow punches only, withdraw as soon as the blows connect, the force coming from the wrist and not the arm. A good pummelling must sing cracking pleasure to the ears. I've said *tam quat* is for the common folk. Our folk like noisy crowds. That's why we fear solitary confinement more than execution. At executions, at least there's gunfire and yelling spectators. This is called patting, your hand forming the dome shape of the tortoise's shell, cupping air and slapping down. You must also make a nice slapping sound. This is the chop, this is a friction rub, this is pinching, pulling, hacking, squeezing, pressing, rolling, they all sound like torture. I've said *tam quat* is not an art of gentle caressing. This is called catching the mouse. Along the back, here and here, under each side of the ridge, there hides a mouse, you have to flush it out to make it run like this. This is called the march of a thousand ants. Use the tips of your fingers lightly, but the customer must feel the goose-pimples rising if you're any good at it. But many customers have backs that are as broad and thick as a divan, and marching ants are nothing, in which case we have to resort to using our fingernails to dig into the flesh like a cricket burrowing its nest and then maybe they'll feel something. Those people love nothing more than a good pummelling. Now this is called the wading stork: your fingers walk like the deliberate and rhythmic feet of a stork. Take your time and don't rush. You can also call it the pecking stork, pecking in single strokes, in a leisurely and unhurried manner. A flurry of typist finger strokes may cause the customer to feel he's reaching the height of pleasure, but that'll be no good. The height of pleasure must be when it hurts the most, the waves of pain followed by a moment of feeling faint and then, a few seconds later, pleasure hits at its most extreme. And this is called the horizontal snake roll. I've told you, *tam quat* is savage and beastly. Marching ants and pecking storks, catching the mouse and rolling the snakes; no dragons and phoenix here. These terms are down to earth but they grate on your ears the first time you hear them. Snake rolls are just the way we roll the skin. There are five places on our body where you can do this: both elbows, both knees and the back. A good roll is when the skin rolls along, one spot chasing another like waves. And now, the height of pleasure, it's simply called plucking. You start plucking here at this spot of the back, and move down, all the way to the coccyx, like this.'

The master changed his position so fast I didn't have time to panic. By now he was bent over me completely, his fingers feeling my backbone from my waist, gripping the skin and plucking hard. With each pluck my back made a cracking sound and it sang a series of notes as his hands moved further and further down. I trembled in silence. Another sound, another and another then he would reach that mole. It took months of total intimacy for my husband to discover the existence of this mole, right there at the hidden spot at the base of my spine, the coccyx. It's a matter known only to the two of us, it's private and strictly forbidden territory.

By now my husband was so captivated, almost hypnotised, that if the master had mounted his wife he would have found it OK. They probably call this riding a buffalo to pluck rice seedlings. The master actually climbed over me. I have seen *tam quat* practitioners sitting astride their customers' buttocks like this before. So these moves and positions all followed a certain script. I know my husband likes to act cool, but surely he was going to intervene, surely he was not going to allow his wife to go that far, my thighs ending up on the master's shoulders like I've seen at some kerbside *tam quat*.

But the two men were engrossed in their task, with one patiently explaining everything and the other listening with such intensity, drinking in every word. For almost a year, my husband had not listened to anyone like this. I almost passed out when the master's four fingers circled the mole and the last sound cracked in a low soft tone.

In the middle of the night I woke up to find my husband straddling my back, loving and gentle, passionate and crazy, a gigantic crawling ant, a pecking stork and a slithering snake all at once. So I had worried unnecessarily over a mole the size of a pea.

On the day that I shed my silk blouse, but kept my bra on, an idea occurred to my husband and he replaced the electric lights with candles. This was on my account, to provide me with a sense of privacy, because as far as the poor master was concerned lighting made no difference. And he was right. The master calmly took hold of my naked back, taking minute care of it like previous times, giving my neck and shoulders his every attention. As for me, my pleasures seemed to permeate even more deeply and my husband probably enjoyed watching his wife's body bathed in the soft candlelight.

Many days later, my husband asked me to remove my bra as well because the straps around the neck and the middle of the back got in the way of the master's hands, spoiling his smooth movements. In addition, by now, my back was so smooth and my neck was almost tension-free, but my chest and abdomen had yet to feel the touch of his hands. My husband feared that if we didn't remind him the master might gloss them over, so he insisted that the master show him the manoeuvres for the front half of the body. The master firmly refused. My husband resorted to sulking, saying, 'So I see you're bound by social taboos like everyone else, hey! Or do you regard us with such contempt?' The master replied, 'No, I wouldn't say that. You are one in a million, Mr Teacher, who dares to live your own way. Nobody would treat you with contempt, and even if they did, it wouldn't worry you. The simple truth is that we have had no experience in handling women, and we don't want our inexperience to give us a reputation of clumsiness.'

My husband tried a provocative tack. 'Oh, men or women, aren't we all humans? If even a person like you would discriminate then what hope is there for equality? I had thought that you and I had agreed on this at the beginning.' As my husband was so insistent, the master reluctantly agreed, on one condition. 'OK, but if we mishandle things a bit, you must forgive us, Mr Teacher.'

How could the master's sure hands mishandle things? These are the hands that rolled my fingers, caressed my feet without neglecting a square millimetre, fingers that never actually touched our sacred spot, always just surrounding it and letting it go, circling and teasing, those fingers that pulled bunches of my hair to make a ticking sound off the scalp, grabbing exactly twenty-nine—my age—strands of hair at a time, the hands that pulled my ears so hard and crisp that it made such a sharp cracking sound, never making a mistake at any of the seventy-eight spots of my body capable of making a sound, those hands that sliding under my armpits always stopped so marvellously close to the base of my bulging breasts. Hands are the eyes of the blind: ten fingers are ten eyes.

Now those hands were hugging my abdomen, then spreading themselves over my belly, fanning across my sides, investigating and probing before determinedly circumventing around my navel. Then with one hand in pursuit of the other, he began a circular rubbing motion that became an ever widening divergent motion, with one hand veering towards the lower abdomen while the other waded up towards the chest area. Then his hands sweetly rubbed hard against my skin with a lot of friction along the bones of the ribcage. Then again and again they rubbed along that narrow strip from my neck to my sternum, taking care to avoid my breasts, squeezing their way in between. My husband thought they were in the master's way, so he took hold of the nipples and parted them to make more space. Then I couldn't tell whose hands were whose anymore.

Then one day my husband told me to discard my pants so that the master could show him with clarity the misalignment of the curved spine. If left untreated, this condition can cause backaches in mild cases, and in severe cases can cause disruptions to periods and even early menopause, my husband said, having looked this up in a book. The diagnosis of my condition was confirmed, the slackness of my left side causing tension on my right side. My husband confirmed that his wife had exhibited all the symptoms, especially the tendency to be picky with food, constipation, being prone to colds and flus, and difficulty sleeping. If the master did not have the courage to treat his wife, he would do it himself. But the master must advise him, must give a demonstration for him to follow. The master hesitated, then said, 'You are a book person, Mr Teacher. Everything you do is underpinned by theories you read in books, you can attribute success or failure to theory. We, as mere practitioners, can base our practice only on our own experiences. Our success or failure depends on lucky chances. We really wouldn't dare invade the territory of the sciences. We would like to retreat.' But by now my husband was quite used to this verbal game of tug-of-war. He knew he would prevail in the end, no matter how complex and ambiguous the master's arguments might be. Deep down, he had even begun to feel a certain kind of disdain for the master, dismissing the way he crafted his circular arguments and the way he pretended to be humble—which served to accentuate his virtues—as typical traits of the useless Asian style of discourse. Yet he took delight in catching the master out and gaining the upper hand. This time, my husband replied quite brusquely, 'Look, Master, if you were the type who would be happy to work the street, I wouldn't have bothered to ask you home. You and I have a common problem. We are ambitious and secretive. We hold others in contempt but we fear being laughed at by the same people we despise. If you allow a small task of realigning a curved spine to defeat you then what are the chances of realigning the stars of fate, realigning the affairs of the world?'

The master protested, 'Aya, to realign the stars you'll have to ask someone else, Mr Teacher.' My husband grasped at the master's words, 'OK, but for straightening a curved back, you've got to help me, OK?' The master nodded in agreement. By now, the two men knew each other very well. They talked to each other in this manner because they liked to hear each other's words, and the more they could anticipate the other's arguments and ideas the more pleasure they derived from the conversation.

The master took the lead and my husband followed. He was clumsy. The master's knees felt soft when pressed against my back. In contrast, my husband's knees felt like a pair of heavy pestles. The master had finished my thigh on this side quite some time ago, but my husband was still struggling, not quite finished. My leg, placed over his shoulder, had gone a little numb. And how could he finish? He had insisted that I wear the pair of underpants embossed with the initials of our names. Maybe the master could decipher our initials by touch and feel. The master showed him the difficult manoeuvres. Massaging the muscles of the pelvic floor, rotating the hips. My husband grasped very quickly all those complex moves, even putting forward his own propositions that sounded quite scientific about collapsed discs, arthritic hips and exercises of the pelvic floor.

But with the simple moves, such as cracking my back, he was hopeless. He held on to my waist, bit at the nape of my neck and mauled my breasts, but my back did not make a sound. The master, on the other hand, simply sat firmly behind my back, supporting me with his knees, his chin resting lightly on the nape of my neck, his arms circling under my armpits around the shoulders, fingers firmly locked together. Then the master gave a gentle push and my back sang a series of beautiful notes. My body arched backwards, my feet in the air hovering above but not quite touching the mat, and my head falling to rest on his chest. The master bent forward, his cheek touching my cheek for a moment, his mouth mine for a second. His hands slowly and quietly let go of the shoulders, catching the falling breasts in the process. Slowly my breasts swelled, my two nipples perked up shamelessly. The master said, '*Tam quat* is quite tactless and inelegant, please forgive my clumsiness, Mr Teacher.' Then he calmly continued to massage with circular, deliberately slow movements. Gradually, I sank into his chest, and I could hear the calm even beats of his heart. Can he visualise what I look like? Maybe he can only feel that women's bodies are just like men's, with a few extra curves? Does he feel any affection towards me, and how can his heart beat so calmly? Is he doing this to give me pleasure or to please my husband?

For more than one month, *tam quat* became our passionate ritual, my husband diligently tidying up the house, rolling out the mat, burning incense and lighting candles. I'd take a bath, spray a little perfume on myself and then the master would arrive at eight o'clock on the dot. In October, it was dark at eight o'clock. In the soft candlelight, the three of us became one. My husband was badly hooked; it was never enough for him. He even felt that my underpants, embossed with our initials, were in the way. 'Every other area of your body has enjoyed this pleasure unhindered, why does this part of your anatomy have to be deprived,' he asked me. How a piece of clothing can hinder the pleasure to a part of my body I don't know, but if taking it off pleased my husband then take if off I would. Again I closed my eyes and rested my shoulders on the master's chest like the other times, but the master's hands came to a sudden stop halfway through. The master gave an involuntary start, I sensed, followed by a sudden but reluctant release of his grip, half wanting to let go, half wanting to hold firm. I held my breath. Did the master feel uneasy because my breasts had swollen too much? Were they spoiled too much today? Or did the master forget for a moment that he was sitting on a mat in the middle of a *tam quat* session? The *tam quat* mat is a place for torture, where the body is to be given a pummelling and then left alone. Brutal and barbaric. Or sophisticated? But the master paused a little too long and when I opened my eyes I could see my husband looming between my thighs.

I don't know whether I sat up or the master pushed me off. Or did my husband yank me away from the master's grip? It happened so quickly and crazily that I am not sure what took place. What could I say to put my husband's mind at peace? The master gave a start; what did he sense? What did he hear, what did he smell? Or what did he see that changed his attitude? How come he stopped so suddenly midway through a session? Why did he turn his head away for a fleeting moment when my husband began to love me? My husband is a very tactful man. Even at the moment of release he's quiet, as if nothing is happening. If the master had not seen, heard or felt something, why did he get a little rattled? He left in a huff, like a man with an injured pride, left while the candles were still burning, saying not a word.

The following day my husband decided not to light any candles. It got dark. My husband said, 'If he really is in the realm of darkness then to him darkness is light. Let's find out if this master of *tam quat* is just sharp of wits or also sharp of eyes.'

I lay there, safely cocooned in the comforting darkness, feeling compassion for my husband but unease for the master. I prayed that the master's world was truly darkness, limitless darkness stretching to the point of hopelessness, and that my husband would be spared of his distress. Spared of having to trace in his mind the master's moves, every one of which now caused my husband acute pain. Didn't the master avoid our secret mole a little too adroitly? Didn't he give the pubic bone just so much attention? Didn't he get to know my body, from head to toes, like the back of his hand? No need to retrace the words that the master used, words that my husband drank with a mixture of anticipation and emotion, but were now coming back to haunt him. Didn't the master say one day, 'One spot chasing another like waves'? Waves are things you cannot describe without seeing. Didn't he also say, 'Your hand should be cupped like the shell of a tortoise'? Has the master ever seen a tortoise? What about ants? Storks? Snakes? But didn't he say, 'Fate had dictated us to be like this and we have to oblige'? What did he mean? 'To be like this' is to be like what? True, he did say, 'People of darkness like us'. But he said people of darkness; he didn't say blind people. This bastard chose his words so cleverly, full of double meanings, laden with ambiguities and impossible to pin down. He was not leery but tactless and clumsy. He did not grope your wife's breasts, but mishandled them. Each day he 'accidentally' pushed against your wife's buttocks and spread your wife's thighs wide open a couple of times. And the curved spine! He could see through every millimetre of your wife's body and yet he said, 'Not so sure'.

Accusing the master of deception would be like calling public attention to our stupidity. Asking around would simply make people laugh. They'd say that out of ten of those who wear dark glasses and work at *tam quat*, fortune-telling, busking or begging, nine are faking their blindness. Real blind people usually pursue wholesome lines of work such as making toothpicks, basket weaving, shelling peanuts or paring onions. Nobody would know who the master was from our description. No names. With such a difficult temperament, he could have been an out-of-work portrait artist, wandering around speaking in that disdainful manner. Once the bastard even hinted that he wanted to follow a different line of work. What kind of work? Sketching realist charcoal portraits? That line of work requires an eye for detail. Now my husband was in an impossible quandary. That's what you get for becoming familiar with the common people. The master's vision impairment was fake but my husband's judgement impairment was real. He poured his heart out and I bared all my flesh. Darkness descended and enveloped both of us. In the dark, the blind can see better than the sighted.

The master did not arrive at eight o'clock. Nor at nine o'clock. The darkness was tense. My husband said nothing. The house was untidy, furniture lay haphazardly arranged. Anyone who tripped over the furniture would fall over the bottles and jars on the tables. I lay in tense anticipation, just like in those nights of my childhood waiting to catch sight of ghosts. This time I would not fall asleep waiting. In November, the nights are long. Nine out of ten may well be fakes, but I didn't care. I counted on the master being the one out of ten who is genuinely blind. My husband usually possesses a healthy scepticism of the opinion held by the majority, preferring the perspicacity of the visionary minority, but on this occasion he seemed to have gone along with the nine out of ten majority. The night was still young and I still invested my trust in a pair of eyes worthy of impairment. I prayed that the master was blind. Blind in a clear, perceptive and proud manner. A blindness that would make things easier for the master and bring relief for everyone else involved. Genuinely blind, permanently blind, without any hope of regaining sight. Blind as though his eyes had been gouged out. Blind so that my husband could be grateful for a special friendship, so that the master could continue to be a special guest in our home. He can even be blind from this day onward, I thought; it's never too late. I will act as his guide taking him anywhere he needs to go. I know my way around. I have waited to the point of ripeness. But why is the master not coming, stepping around things with his easy gait like every other day, so that I can again sink my head into his chest?

I can't remember how many days I waited. I can't remember how much torture was dished out to me in the *tam quat* sessions that my husband continued to give me until my body became a bag of bloody bruises and swollen flesh. And when there was nowhere left unbruised on the misshapen bag of flesh that was me, my husband did not touch me anymore. Then he also left, without a word, just like the *tam quat* master.

Translated by Ton That Quynh Du. An earlier translation appears in Pham Thi Hoai's short story collection, Sunday Menu, *translated by Ton That Quynh Du, and published by Pandanus Books in 2006.*

Pham Thi Hoai is one of Vietnam's most influential writers. Her first novel *Thien Su (The Crystal Messenger)* was published in Hanoi in 1988. It has been published in ten languages, winning the Frankfurt Literaturpreis and the Victorian Premier's Literary Award. She has written another novel, short stories, a children's novella and essays, and has translated into Vietnamese the work of Jorge Amado and Friedrich Dürrenmatt. Pham Thi Hoai lives in Berlin.

Energy as Essence

The Art and Poetry of Basil Eliades

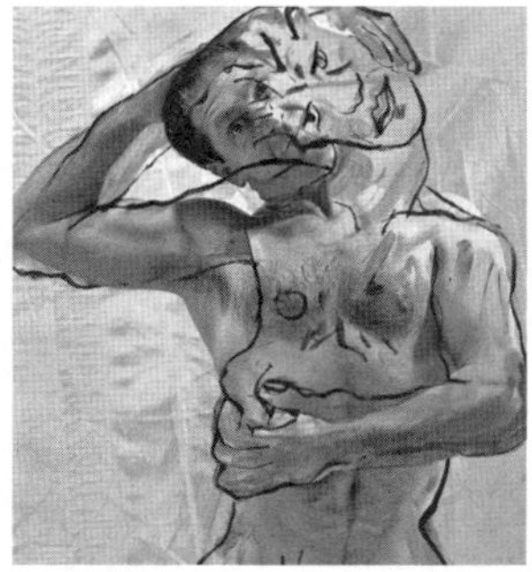

I am more interested in the energy of a word, of an object, than the shape of it. For me, essence is more essential than form. That is why text should be big enough to fill one's mouth, and the experience of reading it aloud like drinking molten chocolate or having one's shoulders rubbed. The parts of a poem may not mean something logically, but they may well mean something illogically or use a different logic, such as that of the subconscious or dream state. The way a poem is read, or said, or accepted, means as much as the cadence that is written into it.

I am more interested in the energy of an image, of a line, than the rendition of its surface. For me, essence is more essential than form. That is why an image should be big enough to fill one's ears and head, and the experience of reading it aloud should be like being filled with hormones, or having music inserted in your spine. The parts of a painting may not mean something logically, but they may well mean something illogically, or use a different logic, such as that of the subconscious, or dream state. The way an image is seen, or accepted, means as much as the cadence that is painted into it.

By saying that 'essence is more essential than form' I don't mean that energy and its source are of more importance than the result—the image or text. Neither works without the other; neither exists without the other. Each is determined by its relationship with the other. The container is as essential as the 'negative' space within it. Neither follows the other; they

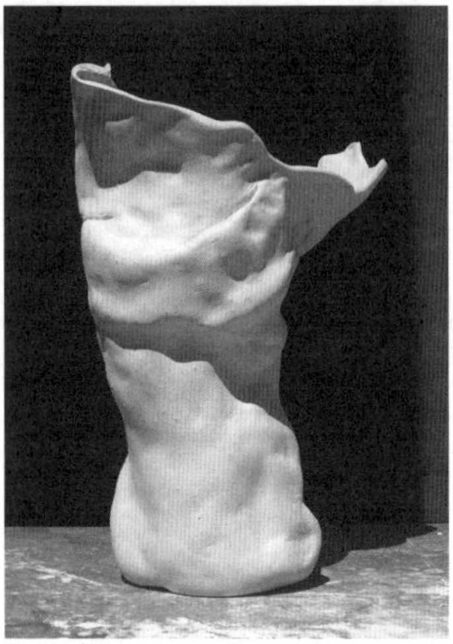

dance, like yin/yang, in perpetual motion. Every word, every breath, is related, and every relationship is related because everything is relative. And because nothing exists in isolation, the 'interconnectedness of all things' is a base value of the self, of the within, of the essence that affects all processes.

Poetry and painting and ceramics and, for that matter, cooking or teaching absolutely belong with one another. I see little difference between playing a piano and working with clay; they both require an understanding of energy. And yes, there is technique and skill, to varying degrees, but even then there is little difference. One may as well be kneading clay, kneading dough, or giving a massage. They are programmed into our DNA. All one has to do is listen hard enough with one's fingers, feel the air, know the breeze, and things occur as if by themselves.

There is no experimentation at all in my writing or painting. The form and layout of the work is merely a part of the process, and simultaneously intrinsic to each piece. It is impossible for me to consider form as separate to any other part. Such elements can be observed, analysed, even modified after the fact, but not during the creative act when images or words are danced into being. The term 'experimentation' is foreign to me; I would rather call it the process of being alive, that is the practice of writing, of drawing, of exploring interactions and the energy that words and images carry. *Exploring* is vital; it is what we need to do, otherwise we become stagnant. My writing, teaching, learning, painting, even my parenting I try to approach with a fresh vision each day, with each interaction. Of course I fail, repeatedly—but I keep trying.

My visual practice informs my text, just as my reading of text, of image, of social dynamics, of philosophy, of anything, informs my visual art practice and my every interaction with the world. A useful example is how I came about writing the poem titled *Why*. I was in Melbourne, sitting at a small table at a street-side café, with my thoughts turned inward. A woman walked past and for an instant I had a sense of a silent communication with her, her energy vibrating with mine. As she swished past I got a rush of information about everything that was happening, at that moment, in that whole block. The city was downloading, and I was its channel. I heard, saw, smelt, felt, and understood, in an instant, the rock beats thudding through car walls and how they shoved awkwardly against the music floating out of a shop nearby, people kissing, a dozen arguments, food being made and masticated and swallowed, shadows and suits and phones and advertising and scoliosis, and I felt it all and the poem was there, instantly. It then took some months of re-working, but it was fully there, incarnate.

That moment, or rather 'the' moment, is the moment of openness to reception. That moment was a composite spark, setting the creative process in motion. That moment was a portal to my perceptions and reception. If the moment can be a portal, a title is like a door handle. It offers an opportunity to grasp the energy of a subject, or concept, or spatial relationship, and sit with it for a moment. After that, one can step through the door and grapple with or free-fall into the poem or image. The works tend to choose their titles themselves, self-electing, but sometimes it's a struggle. Especially with poetry, because a title is necessarily part of the piece yet separate to it, clarifying its role and isolating, identifying. Choosing a title can be as difficult as writing the poem. So much can depend on that one word and its integrity and responsibility for the appearance of the entire piece. The title also has to counterbalance the energy of the entire piece, which is so often a big ask.

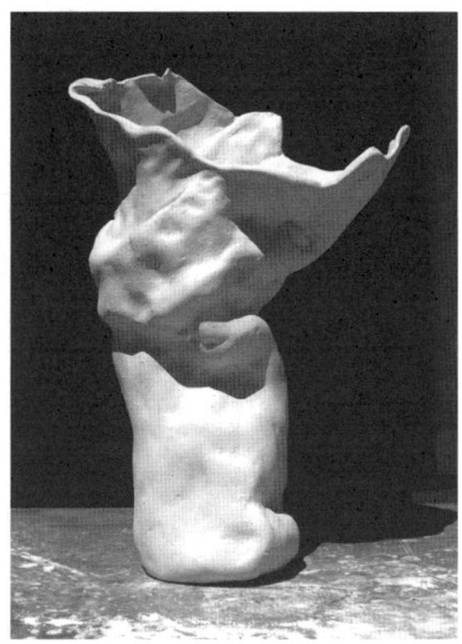

But that kind of information flow doesn't necessarily make writing or painting or what is happening internally any easier for me, but I'm grateful for the insights and am slowly getting better at controlling and articulating them. That control means that I am less likely to be overloaded by information, and so I am more able to be in my centre and less reactive to other images and energies. I feel it is a holistic way of seeing, which for me means seeing conceptually, experientially, in 3D, in 2D, in time and space, and energetically. It is also often profoundly confusing when what I see or hear or feel seems to contrast so dramatically with what others are experiencing.

For me, the idea of seeing at many levels and from a multitude of angles is what it means to be doing art and to be living. And it is all-encompassing and affects everything I do—every move, every relationship, every creation.

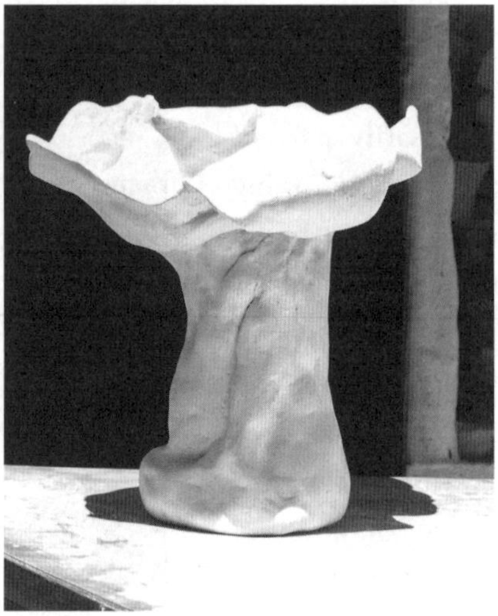

Being and Non-Being

On cai me on—Aristotle
For AD, hope.

This evening two divine beings of light
being so flight
Ate supper,,
dissolved into fight,
Recovered, and then bid bye.

The enemy undivided,
The esteemed tide of logic tilted and turned
Now sways in its own constructions
Weeping into unintended, untranslatable emotions,
& the rough inscription of inadvertent violence,
hatched from unwise weddings and graceless revolutions.
The opera of breakfast
The hundred meter dash of lunch,
The miscalculation of dinner,
And poorly calibrated kisses
God, send me soon a lover or two,,
fit for the dreams of gods, of whom I dream,
Now my hands tire of hailing
And my heart, of healing yours,
But of mine, green and gracious under apple boughs
wants to the extravagance of young shared breath
ope's to my sporadic whims and intransigent resolutions,
and these words, grailed, in venice and venetian light
translate,
while our daughters stoop to scoop light from their ankles
Throw diamonds to the skies
Dance through a raining shower of kisses,

And collapse into the snow safe blanket.
        It is lovely to read this,
        Though I shan't.
I love me.
        I love me.
I am the most uniquest thing.
No-one ever saw so many slow
extrusions of change.
        Yes,
        you articulate the choreography
        of your own hard won evolution.
You dance with text, climb inside it,
Straining possibility with each phrase,
Creating a new you.
        The breadth of your character
        motivates the breath of your characters.
Simple tools, well wielded,
Freeze, desiccate, sculpt, melt,
organise air and manipulate
the supple doubt of outsiders (& we all are)
Until we see ourselves, anew.
From our penitentiaries of private doubt
we are inducted into happenings of growth.
        Can you see who you can be?
There is a delight in being me.
        And so I emerge
        as Autumn unwraps itself,
        A glorious gift of attrition.
It is the taste, the magnificence
the salty understanding of the scale and vastness of a word,
on the tongue   in the mouth
temporarily orally fixated   open throat,
'connect with me!'
        I belong elsewhere.

There is only ever here.
        Divide one cell by sonic fusion
        And you get nuclear winters
there is no need for maps, a direct connection exists
in all directions and dimensions,
travelling from b to a
is as easy as growing a limb;
it has already happened.
        I have, so deeply, danced into depression
        Tripped over our children
        who dance along a path in verbal velvet,
and We, grappling under skies, fighting over boundaries and fences,
        Loosely received, relieved
When you say you you mean i
When you say i you mean you.
        I count the words with which flattery fawns,
        empty of emptiness,
        holding the space between our conceptions,
        for my inactive other to be born.
Quiescent, Nascent,
I will be a footing for my own growth,
I will anchor me like a bridge.
        To hold everything that I am
        And you are.
Aphrodite, Eve and Jezabel
All of you have I loved
        He stands by you in your chaos
To stand by you in your chaos.
        I have adopted an incarnation,
        radiant with guile,
        requiring the workings of my face
        to be digested daily.
Men cry empty floods, our weak skin harmed
& ask for vision.

We drink oceans, and, beneath memories,
swim after random whispers
we see in our delirium, urge the tranquil tensioned night
toward absurd fear and pain
and flatter the dismal sun.
          We do not change; we cope.
          I am my own worst enemy
          and i follow me to the grave.
I sing the endurance of my heart,
Heart working the words,
Words working the world into a small ball,
an undesirable amassing of moments alone.
I sing the moment alone.

& loud.

A biographical note by Pin Affleck

BASIL ELIADES is a person, painter, poet, parent, partner and teacher. He has a great deal of fun dragging himself and anyone else into understandings of philosophy as a viable means of existence. His works are powerful and pleasurable, and his readings are a literary gymnasium where lines dance off his tongue marrying together with such gusto and burning with emotion one sits paralysed by the sheer energy, let alone the images. His third poetry collection *3rd i* was released by I.P. in 2006. The audio+text-active CD is being released in March, 2007, also by I.P. Go to www.basileliades.com

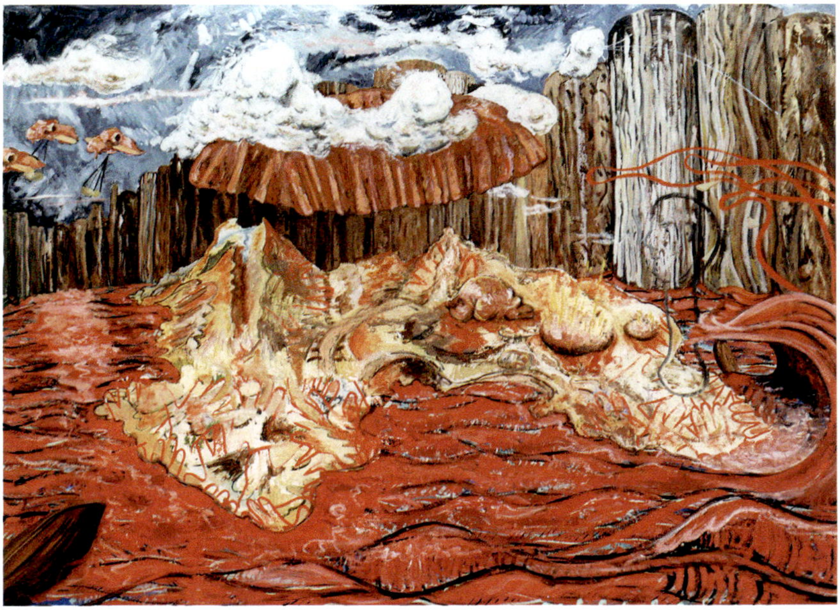

Bloody Island Mentality (Where second-hand Europeans pullulate / Timidly on the edge of alien shores), 2002, 167.5 x 237.5 cm.

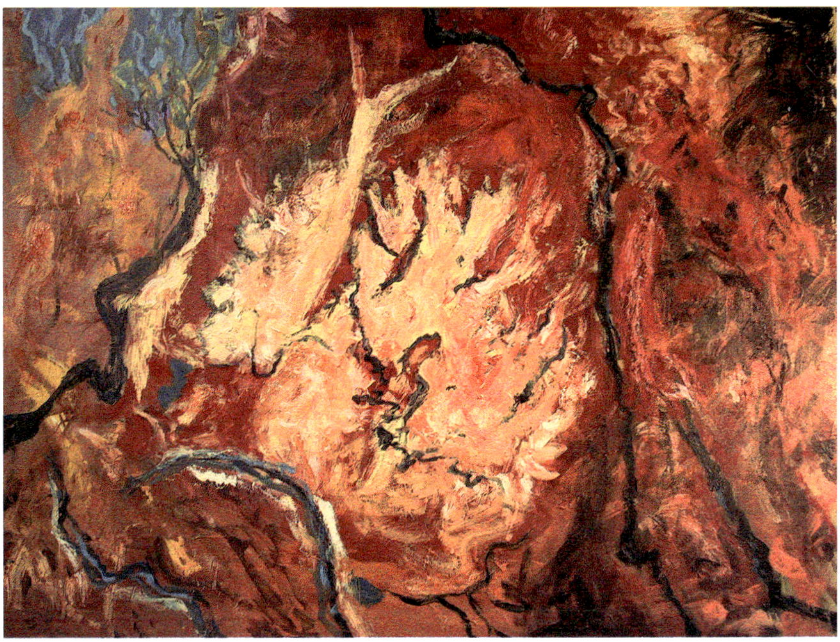

Satellite #1, 2005 , 107 x 137 cm.

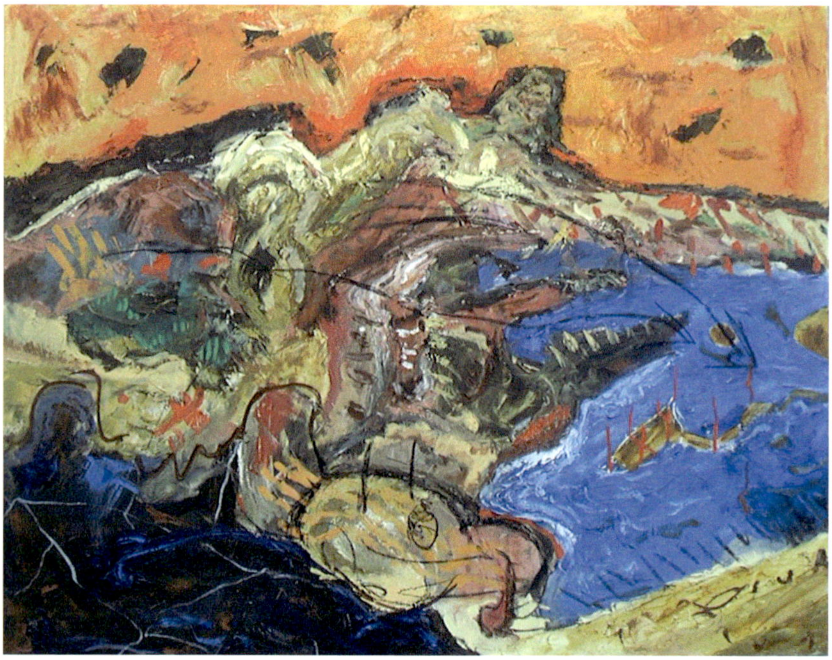

Macro/Micro, Swedish Archipelago, Ballarat, 2001, panel one, 107 x 137 cm.

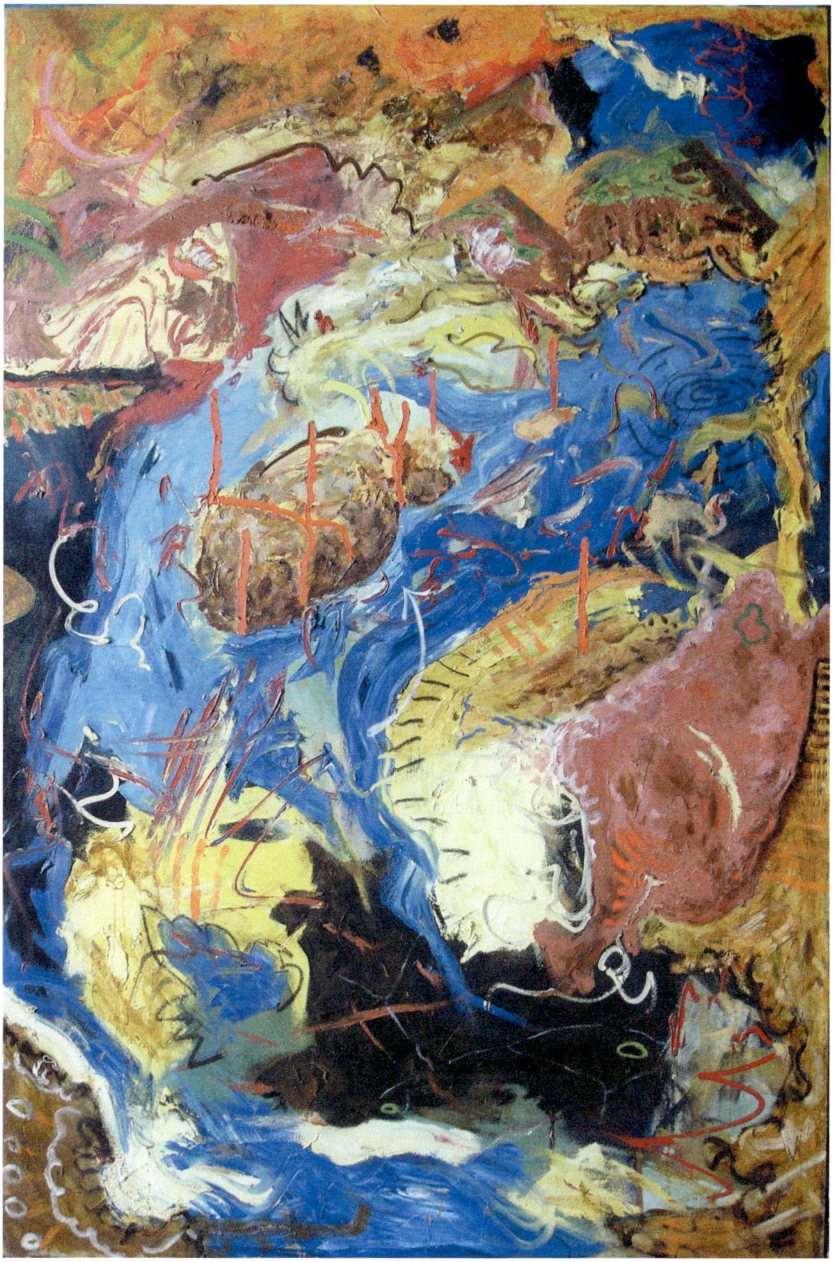

Macro/Micro, Swedish Archipelago, Ballarat, 2001, panel two, 184 x 121 cm.

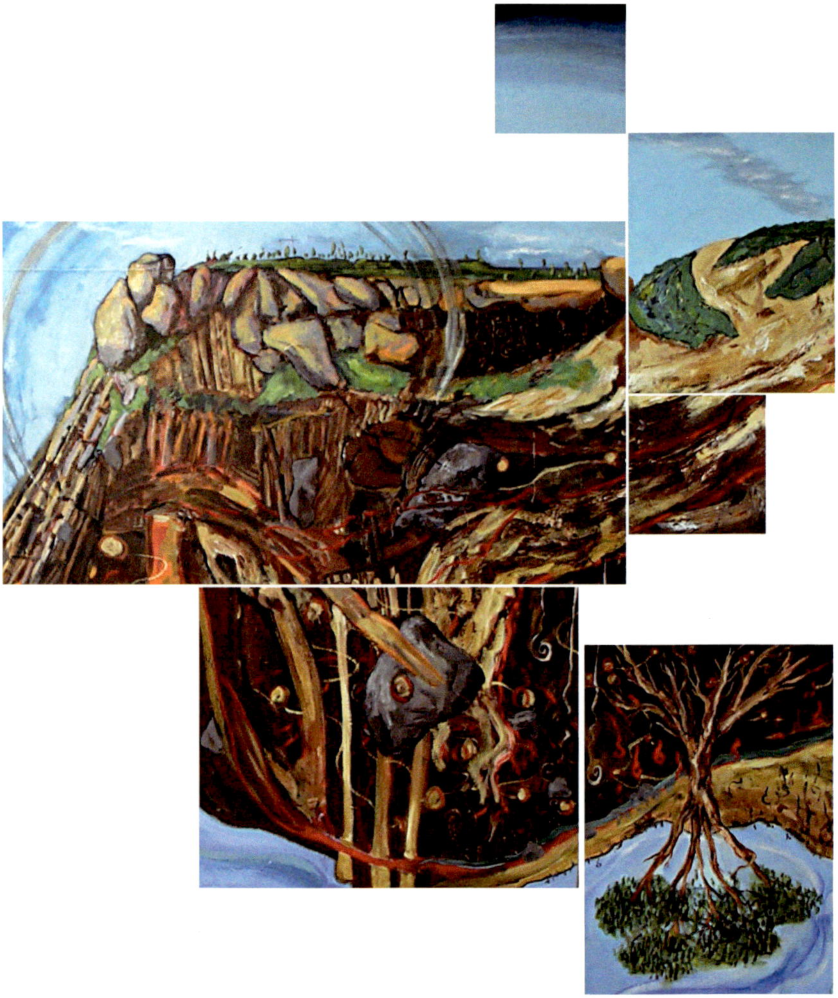

Detail from *Infinity #1*, 2005. Polyptych, 17 panels, 210 x 500 cm (overall), oil and charcoal on canvas and linen, negative spaces, bird frame, hollow, wood.

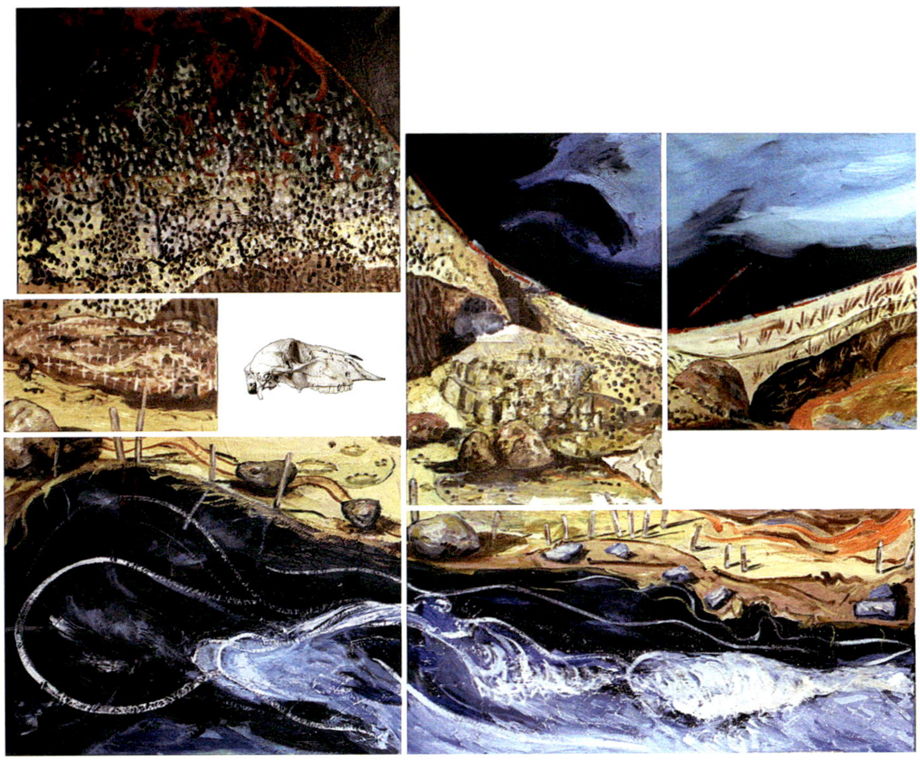

Detail from *The River of Her Immense Stupidity*, 2002. Polyptych, 17 panels, 250 x 700 cm (overall), oil, sand, charcoal, photographs on canvas and linen, negative spaces, sheep's skull.

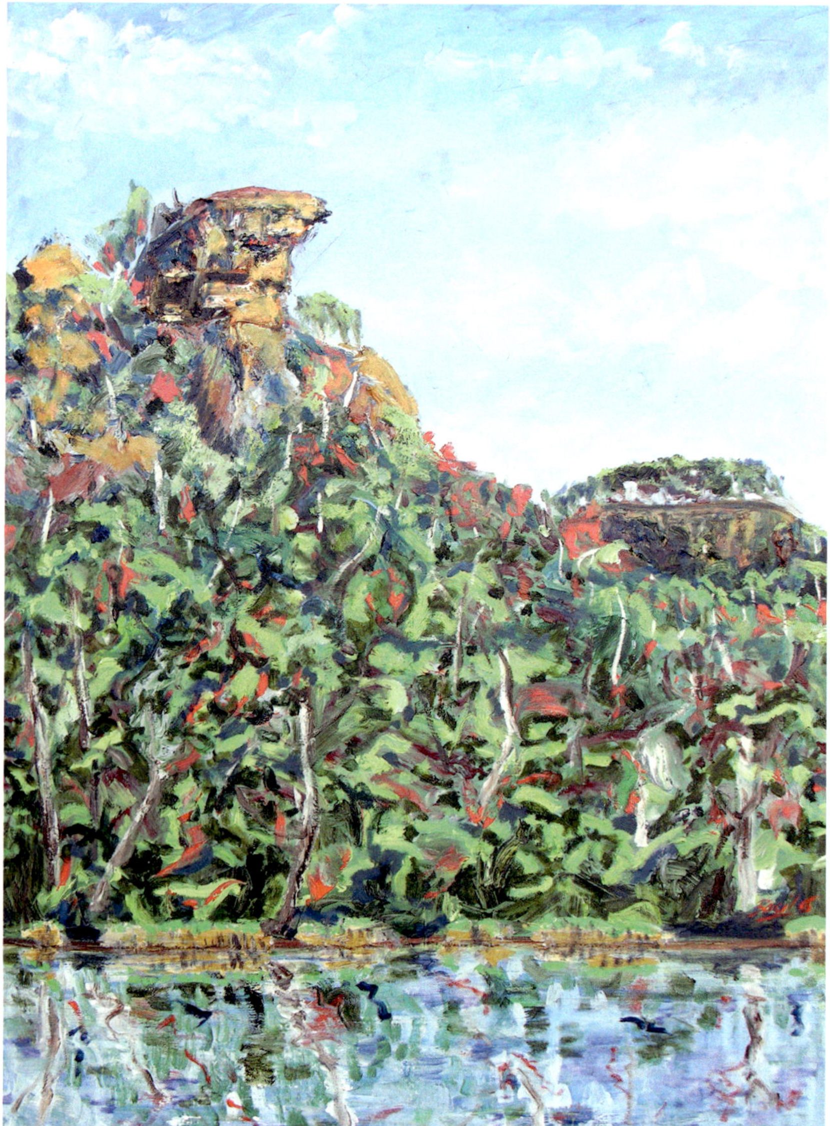

Pulpit Rock, 41°, 2005, 157 x 111 cm.

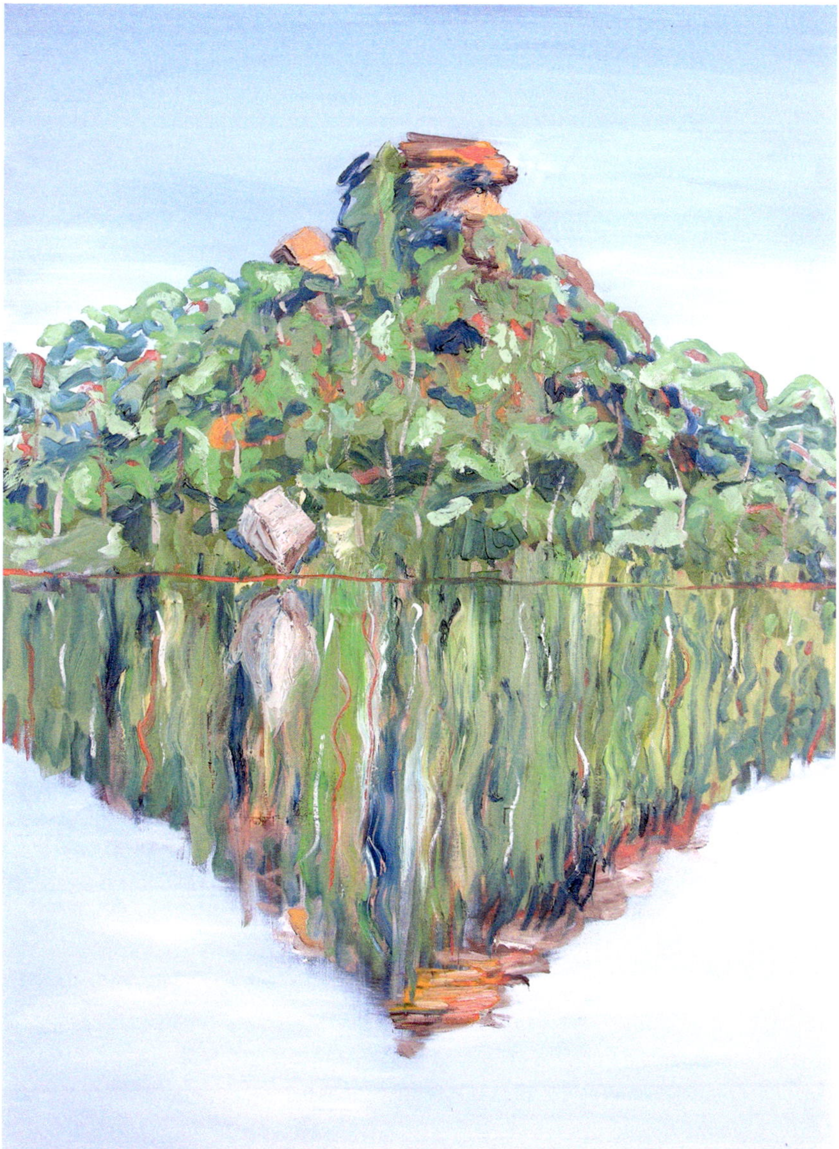

Bundanon Suite 014, 2005, 120 x 90 cm.

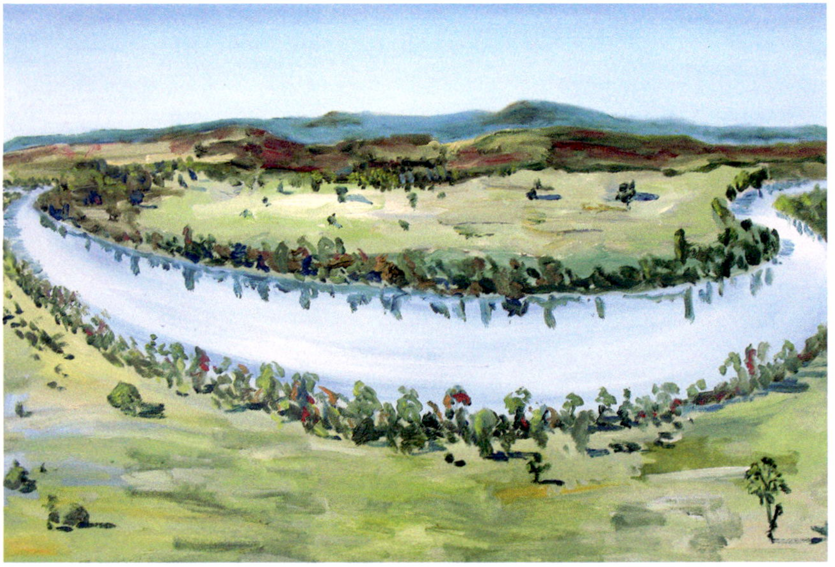

Bundanon Suite 017, 2005, 66 x 91 cm.

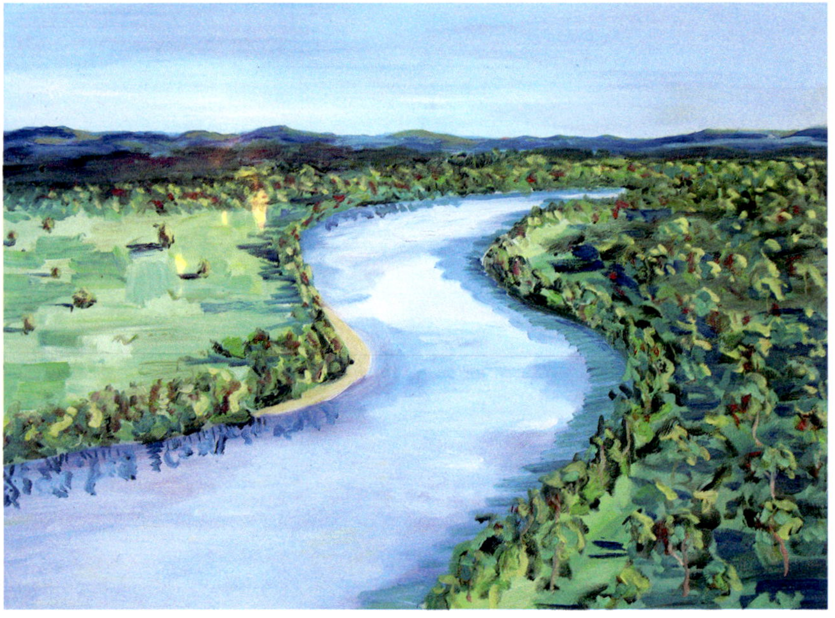

Bundanon Suite 002, 2005, 66 x 91 cm.

THE DEVIL AND THE RIVER

CHRISTINE STANTON

Morning

Sometimes I hear the river moan; a half-hour ride beyond the trees it pulls its heavy waters from the west and pours toward the coast. Marion says it's edged with mud, and fenced with reeds stiff and hollow as mutton shank bones.

'Look,' she says, and shows her basket made of river reeds. 'It's only us moans, not the river. The river doesn't feel the heat. The heat brings us to sighs and faints and late-day walks in the garden yard.' She pulls long stalks of lavender from the hedge along the path where we are walking through the parched and dying garden. 'There ...' she says. 'See? Like this, bend and weave them so, to make soft nets to prison fairies in.' She drops her voice and looks sidelong at me. 'This is how the blacks do,' says Marion. She has seen the blacks many times, amongst the river reeds.

She has seen Parramatta too. She has seen barges bump the wharf and take on loads of wool. She has waved them down the river and watched the speckled ducks bob in their wake on the water road to Sydney town to meet the sailing ships.

I have not seen this; not any of it. I only have the length of view from house to outer paddocks. Across the paddocks is a hill. Behind the hill the earthen road is travelled to and from towns and homesteads. Our farm track joins it, to take my father there from time to time. I hear the noises of the road sometimes: carts, horses, tired dragging boots, and songs and quarrels. Marion has been along this road and says I could not have heard this, not from this house. She says all this does happen on the road, but too far away for me to hear.

Today we search the vine along the paling fence for any grapes the wasps have left, but find none. All are spoilt and weep a sticky sweetness. It is past true summer, but still too dry to smoke the hard-baked wasp's nest in the eaves.

We watch the sky for signs of storm but only see blue air swirl oily in the heat.

I clutch my hat and tilt my head and spin slow on my heels and see a bowl of sky circled with the tops of trees; the measure of my world. I drop my head and stretch my arms and waltz-turn tiptoe, finger-pointing north, then east, now south, and west. One, two, three, four points for each stone cairn that mark the limits I may walk alone.

These are the rules I must keep to have the life my father says I should aspire to:

I may walk the house-yard anywhere.

I may walk the Close Field accompanied by loud farm dogs and an adult.

I may visit sheds and stables with Janet, and take Marion with me if she's here.

I may walk with Janet through the gate and down the Wattle Path to where my mother's grave is, but never in the heat. Sun cracks the soil and lets miasmas out; best let graves be, in heat.

I may not go into the gully that cuts through the bush beyond the hay shed.

I may run down the brown dirt track to the sounding of my father's horse, if Janet sees the way is clear and I can be watched the whole way to the giant gum.

I may go no further, but must stay here; kept and guarded for a lord.

My father brings me silver, lengths of silk, and journals from the distant world. He brings me books for ladies, on manners, dancing steps and verse.

He brings me pamphlets on *How To Find and Banish Vice In Lady's Maids* from Paris, and how to open fetes.

One season more and he will put us on a ship to find a lord in London, where they are. There are no lords in Sydney town, just rough beasts, half–men, he says. ('And devils, too', says Janet, 'for is not this land a hell?')

My lord will live in cool green woods of oak and beech. He'll set Italian marbles near a lake to please me. We'll stroll down avenues of sycamores, and feed the peacocks on our velvet lawns. My father says so.

Six years ago my governess kissed me goodbye and said, 'God help you, child. This heat, this wretched heat, steals too much life and some men's reason.' I liked her so. We talked a lot. Now I may speak to no one while I'm guarded for my lord, only Janet, and only Hob and Willum when Janet's there to see and hear. And only Marian—who is no one—sent by Mistress Ashley now and then to sweep and wipe about the house, and beat grey dust out of the tight-stretched muslin screens set to thwart the summer sun that burns against our windows.

'Come, Miss,' Marion calls me now. 'Let's gather mint to crush and put in corners to keep the flies away.'

Just one more season, and the grain brings home our passage fee, and I shall see the river and the road. Though I long to see them now, to lean against the road gate and call the wagons halt, have them draw their horses up and talk with me a while.

'How is the town?' I'd say, and, 'Who is there? What do they wear? Who is wicked? Who is good? Are there other girls like me, in Parramatta or in Sydney?'

The men have stripped and bagged the last of grain and stacked it on the dray. Janet walks me to the sheds to see the cart horse harnessed. The bags of grain are warm and scented with the best of summer's pearly barley. I sniff and pat them.

'Smells like your lord then?' Willum says. 'Smells like your towers and marbles? Smells like gold?'

Hob says, 'Ah, no, I say *wools* buys more lords than barley.' He snickers.

'Shush now, sly thing,' Janet warns him.

But Hob mutters, 'Always the wools brings back most gold.'

The grain goes down the road today, and I have one more year behind the trees that screen the river, the hill that hides the road.

I turn to Janet.

'I hear laughing on the road. I hear them travel happily. If I call them will they hear me?'

'Only hear of you in gossip,' Willum says.

'Shush you, Willum!' Janet slaps him, then waves away a fly and says, 'God take this unkind summer, and put an English autumn in its place.'

Afternoon

'Marion,' I say. 'Leave the pillow hems unsewn today and sit and help me paint you.'

We settle in the parlour. I spread a cloth, and on it put tiny china troughs of aquarelles, and wet my brushes in a glass of water from the kitchen pail.

'Don't frown. I want your copy fair and smiling, Marion,' I say. She's glum though, and she sighs.

'I would not have you go, Miss. Who would I ever be with then, but Miz Ashley, who is hard and mad for money? And who would be a mirror to the world for you?'

'Silly girl,' I say. 'You'll have a husband too, some strong assigned man who has earnt his freedom and got a piece of land.'

'No,' she says and shakes her head.

'Be still! Look, Marion, you made me let loose a drop of colour on my dress.'

'Sorry, Miss, but perhaps you should not wear a white dress while you're painting.'

'White is most suitable for ladies in the summer, Marion. Especially if they are still waiting for their love.'

I wipe my brush, and bid her hold her head in profile.

'And how will you know love?' she asks. 'Miz Ashley says you've never seen a man but servants and your father, and would think any new young man to be a lord.'

'You have a bold mouth, Marion, and I shall paint it so.'

The paintbrush rings against the glass and stains the water umber from the sun in Marion's skin.

'This water from the house-yard pump, Marion? Is this the same that makes the river? Are all waters one?'

'I don't know.'

'Do not shrug your shoulders, girl. It shifts your head and spoils the line I want to paint.'

She stares towards to the looking glass that's opposite the window. It's meant for holding light in here on dull days, but in this shrouded summer room it mirrors only Marion's face, her lids half down to hide her look.

'Miz Ashley says you're better left here, where no harm comes.' She sighs. 'Nor no pleasure either ... though that's a thing gone quick. Miz Ashley thinks you should be shown the sheep at tup in springtime, so you'll not think pink roses and pale ribbons is all there is to being wed. She says you should be told before you go that lords might like your gold, but some like other lords as much as they like ladies.'

'I will not hear this talk,' I say, severe, as ladies must be. I know all servants talk in riddles, they have no education. But I have learning, and in one quick start I do believe I've spied within my mind the riddle of all waters.

I know this is an island land, and I've heard that there are islands in the river too, where it spreads wide and tastes of salt as it comes close to Sydney town. Perhaps all lands are islands, yet adrift upon the sea, but so big and heavy that we think them held on mighty stems of rock rising from the solid heart of Earth. In truth, I think we float, slow but certain, about a watery globe. Yes, I am sure of this and wonder why others do not seem to know it, when they have seen the sea and I have not.

I shake the paintbrush and grey drops of aquarelle, for Marion's eyes, fall on the tablecloth and sprinkle on my skirt.

'These drops of water are the same that come from out the flood that floats the world, that makes the rivers and the ponds and wells and all the oceans that the ships sail on,' I say.

'Well, then, Miss,' says Marion, 'if you wait, then time will float this land to England and you can take but one step from dust to cobbles and never have the danger of a journey.' She jumps up suddenly. 'Take me with you, Miss! I know best which man is honest and which likes lies. You've only seen their copies drawn, primped to prettiness as you are making mine. You only know what others wish you to. You have never learnt to read smooth faces for their naughty thoughts.'

'Poor Marion,' I say, and toss my chin and turn my head away, as ladies learn to do, to show reproof. 'There's badness in a servant's world, but not in mine.'

I know that this is true because there is never any news to read of lords and ladies doing bad.

Evening

At the edge of evening, I held the lantern high at the house yard gate for Marion to see her homeward way along the track into the bush. Although she says she has no fear of dark, nor natives, nor the wraiths of hell, nor things that wait to snatch at passing feet.

She says, 'I stamp the ground each seventh step and sing out loud. The song's that's best are shanties and some London bawdies to keep the Devil in his place away from me.'

'Do you not think that's tempting him to show his hand?' I ask.

'I think ...' she says, and reaches up to hug goodbye and whisper close, 'I think there is no Devil here, it is too far for him to come from the forests of Bohemia.' She laughs and skips away a step as the dogs begin to bark. Like me they have heard the hoofbeats cross the far-off road beyond the trees, though I thought no more of it for my father never rides from that direction.

Then the dogs begin to howl as the scrub beyond the barley field cracks loud, brittle under the weight of a monstrous, snorting, thundering thing that springs across the stubbled ground, raising dandelions of dust.

'Here is the Devil now!' I cry, astonished.

Marion nods and says, 'Come visiting this furnace-land to try its heat against his own.' She claps her hands and laughs to see the Devil run.

The dogs stand up and dance, choking on their chains.

Hob and Willum hurry from their hut, and look which way to go to flee the Devil. Janet flies out of the house and pulls me quick behind her back.

The Devil dances closer now and turns and dips his head to me as he draws up before the house-yard gate. His eye is round and lustrous under its shade of spider-legs. His haunches, belly, chest are burnished in the lamplight—some servant has polished him mahogany. He's strapped in oiled leather, caught piece by piece with shiny rings and buckles fine as any lord wears on his shoes and fingers. The Devil's prouder than a lord is, though the Devil has a master on his back.

'Get, you!' Janet screams.

The Devil rears on slender legs and metal shows curved round his hooves of horn. His master holds close to his flanks.

'Madam, hold your temper! I'm here to save your lives,' he says. 'You should leave at once. There's convicts out and on the way, come from Vinegar Hill. They wish to burn our farms and speed us to our maker. Only bring my mount some water, then I'll take you from here quickly.'

'Marion. Bucket,' Janet says, still shielding me.

'This lady is my charge,' she says. 'She cannot leave here, nor can I. I am promised much for her safety and mean to have that reward.'

'But Madam ...' He leans towards her, and the Devil takes one small step close. Janet strikes her fist against the rider's thigh. He steps the Devil sideways, back, and shorts the reins to hold the Devil's head. Too late, the soft glove-leather mouth shows teeth, and the Devil has bit Janet.

Marion sets the bucket down and lifts a hand to hide her smile.

'Oh Ma'am, I hope the Devil has not sipped your blood too much,' says Marion, and bobs a mocking head to Janet. 'It would be the worse for him.'

She winks at me and runs off down the track, moth-flutter in the dark, until she disappears into the trees along the gully. The Devil drinks from the bucket, then rolls his arched neck high, water dripping from his mouth. He reaches it to me, and I reach too. We are meant to touch each other. His muzzle in my palm is soft and whiskery. He licks my fingers.

'Get that creature off her, or I'll see you shot!' Janet cries.

The rider smiles, sits easy, hands on hips.

He says, 'I see the lady's fond of Arabs.'

'You do *not* see the lady sir, nor she see you,' Janet snaps. 'And she cannot be fond of anyone but her father and the one for whom she is intended. She has no thought for devilish heathen Arabs.'

The rider strokes the Devil's neck, the lovely arc and swoop of it.

'*This* is an Arab, bred here, from Cape stock,' he says. 'He will step you swift away from harm. I'll take you to the river. There are boats already in the stream with soldiers at the oars, and standing armed to take the blacks or convicts.'

'We can't go,' Janet says. 'I'll have no reward if she is done wrong by.'

'Madam, I must leave. I will not burn here with you. Look ...' He points to where two pale shapes, Hob and Willum, are running through the trees.

'There, your men are gone already. They must have heard the news.' He pulls sharp upon the reins, reaches down and grasps my hand.

'Come, Miss, don't be afraid. Hold tight, I'll lift you up and keep you neat within the circle of the reins.' And in a trice, he does.

The Devil has me safe now, my cheek and arms against the muscle of his neck. I feel his pulse beat next to mine as if no skin between us.

'Wait!' says Janet. 'I shall fetch her cloak, it would not do to have her good white dress spoilt, and the night is cold.'

'Hurry then,' the rider says.

Janet brings my grey cloak, draped across her arm. As she hands it up to me, I see a pistol barrel gleam. The Devil's master sees it too. He clucks his tongue.

The Devil wheels and flicks his tail at Janet, who steps back lest it touch her face. She almost drops the pistol, but keeps hold and aims it at the rider, as she snatches at my skirt. She fires wide. The pistol jumps. She fires again, and misses, as the Devil leaps towards the scrub, past the Close Field, past the cairns of stone.

We leave a scrap of ribbon-lace in Janet's fingers.

I must hold tight, so cannot tie my cloak fast about my neck. With every step it loosens more, and the wind, which cleaves before the Devil to let him through, gathers up behind us to pluck the woollen folds. At last the wind claims it and tosses it away, to fall on barley stubble.

Still the wind pushes at our faces, and draws my skirt back tight against my legs, as if to strip me of the moon-white dress that glows against the darkness. I lean into the Devil's neck and feel the silky, winnowing mane flutter on my face. He is a pretty Devil this, who speeds me to the river.

We fly through scrub and under branches. The Devil takes his way so sure-footedly that I think that he must know each inch of the entire world as well as God does.

We reach the road that I have so often longed to travel on. We do not turn along it, but leap across it into more bush, downhill all the while.

The Devil gallops faster, and stretches out his neck.

'You see?' his master cries. 'We're near the river. He gets the smell of it and wants to drink.'

I smell it on the wind too. The smell of many rains, gathered in one long skein of silty water. The vegetable stink of reeds, and tree roots standing in the water.

We slow, and walk the sloping bank downward to the river.

The Devil whickers softly and steps, so careful, to the water's edge. As he dips his handsome head to drink, I lean back gently on his master's breast. His master curves his arm more tightly round my waist, though there's no need. We are so still now that mosquitoes come to buzz around us. And to bite. I slap the stinging places on my hands and face.

The Devil's master slides to the ground and bends to scoop up river mud. He takes my hands, one by one, and dabs mud on them.

'The blacks do this, to keep mosquitoes off,' he says. He pats mud on my face, and smooths it down my neck. Some falls on my dress. We wait, and listen. We hear a rhythmic *thump, click, shssss, thump, click, shssss.*

'What is that noise?' I say, alarmed.

'It is oars you hear. That is the boat to take you downstream to the town, and to safety.'

I peer between in the gaps in a colonnade of eucalypts along the riverbank, beyond dark feathertails of leaves that brush the moon. I see a shaft of light travelling on the surface of the water. It drags a boat behind it.

I see *them*, too. Huddled shapes wrapped in dark cloaks crouching in the centre of the boat, and soldiers rowing. Soldiers standing prow and stern with guns cocked, watching. The soldiers' caps are draped with net, against mosquitoes, as are the hats the shadowy passengers wear.

A soldier standing in the prow holds a lantern with blinkers on its sides, like our carthorse wears, to light a narrow path of trembling gold for the boat to follow. A watching soldier sees us and hails his comrade in the prow, who turns the lantern light towards us as the rowers ship their oars. The sudden light is painful to my eyes. I blink. The dark creatures in the centre of the boat stir and look up. The Devil's master calls to them, he says that I wish to go with them.

The soldiers bring the boat up to the bank. One takes a rope and twines it around a branch, once, twice, three times. Another grasps an overhanging branch to hold the boat fast in the current.

The cloaked figure of a lady stands up in the centre of the boat. She greets me, and I think she smiles at me behind her veil of netting, but I cannot tell for certain. She must see me clearly, though, for the lamplight makes me bright as London journals say the stage is lit at night for operas to play on.

A soldier speaks low to the lady. She turns again to me.

'Do you have a cloak?' the lady asks.

'My cloak is lost.'

'We have no spare cloak here for you,' she says.

'I do not mind. I am not cold.' I do not tell her that though the wind has chilled my skin, I am still warm from riding with the Devil.

'It is not against the cold,' the lady says, 'but to cover your white dress, lest blacks or convicts see us easily and quickly have us dead. I must keep all my charges safe from harm.'

The river's flow is pulling at the boat. The soldier in the prow lowers the lantern so that the light falls away from me, and points again along the water. I can see now my dress holds light as if it shines from my body underneath.

The Devil lifts his heads and snorts. He's drunk his fill and is impatient to be off.

'Madam,' his master says. 'I shall take the lady with me if she does not mind more rough travel through the bush; it is too dangerous to take the road.'

'Yes,' I say. 'Oh, yes.' We wave farewell, although I think I could be easily hid in the bottom of the boat amongst those many cloaks.

All night long we ride along the ridge between the road and the river. We see no convicts rioting. No blacks leap from the shadows with their spears raised. Only the bush contests with us, setting rocks in the Devil's path, clawing at his reins and straps, and flinging branches in our faces; but the Devil keeps his footing and his way.

It almost dawn when we climb a ridge top where the bush shows thin against the sky. I look out and down and see a mighty stretch of water with an opposite shore so far away that trees on it look shrunken.

'The sea,' I shout. 'It is the sea.'

'Not yet,' the Devil's master says. 'This is the river still. Though we're not far from where it takes on salt.'

I think he's wrong, for surely there could never be a river this wide, with banks so distant from each other. I truly think this is the ocean and that far shore is England. I'm sure that I was right to think all lands drift unanchored on the oceans' swell, carried as safe as I am carried on the Devil's back. Though I never thought to see England come so close so soon. I was only wrong to think that continents would move as laggardly as years.

Suddenly it's dawn, and in its light I see my dress is limp and stained with mud, smeared with the Devil's sweat and my own body-damp, and grey-spotted with spilt aquarelle that I had thought would help make Marion's eyes.

The Devil's master says that now we are riding on his own land.

'Is it not fine?' he asks. 'Look, here's a view of the town from the place I will build my house.'

He shows me a small town on a sheltered inlet of the far bank. I marvel at the town, counting half a hundred buildings and twice as many tents. But I see that this cannot be London, for there are too few lights and one could walk the place from end to end within a day and there can be room for only a quarter of the number who live in London town.

I see now that this water might not be the ocean, for there are ships moored at the dock that are so big I think they must be meant for wider, deeper waters than are here.

Perhaps, too, desired lands weigh too heavy and drift too slow to reach us in a single lifetime.

Christine Stanton is a Sydney-based writer and teacher. She has an MA in Writing from the University of Technology, Sydney, and has written for a variety of media. Her short fiction has appeared in *Griffith Review*, *Island*, *Southerly* and *Best Australian Stories 2006*. 'The Devil and the River' was shortlisted for the international 2005 Fish/Historical Novel Society short fiction competition. She has recently completed a novel on the interlocking themes of migration and expatriation.

The Water Way

Guy Kelly

You know, brother, you were in my dreams last night. I was tangled in the mooring rope, overboard, in the canal. Gasping for breath, struggling to untangle myself, I was. Then someone pulled me out of the water. It's been a long time since I saw you last, but I knew it was you, brother. You pulled me close, by my coat, and whispered, 'Joseph, Jo ... why?' before your grip loosened and you disappeared, sending me back into the water. Ambiguous fellow, aren't you? I'd like to think I won't obsess about what you meant; but truth be told it's a lonely life for me now. Still, it won't be long now, Nevan. Won't be long now.

What a beautiful day. Cruising the Grand Union, birdsong rolling playfully in my ears and darting from one tune to another. Face up to the sun on a day like this and he'll reward you with the gentle, warm and silky stroke of his minion, the breeze. Moments of beauty you can feel like this need to be cherished. I know all too well it can be taken from you without so much as a moment's notice. You never realise just how much you take feeling beauty for granted—experiencing it rather than just observing. Whether it is a kind breeze caressing your face on a sunny day or the special embrace only a loved one can give, my advice is simple: take it to heart and appreciate it fully. When my freedom was taken, all I had was memories and hope. Memories of days like these playing as a child back in Monaghan with you; and hope that I would hold Rosaleen again, despite what her father said. Oh, brother. You would have loved Rosaleen.

It's a peaceful life living on the canals, albeit boring on my own sometimes. All I have for company is a crackly old radio that doesn't seem to receive any frequency and the odd person I moor next to. I don't mind too much, though. I've had plenty of time to get used to my own company. As I lay here under the moonlight, outstretched on the narrow boat roof, my thoughts wander back to Rosaleen. Funnily enough, brother, I was flat on my back when I met her for the first time. It was the summer of 1998. I was twenty-two and had been living in Dublin for three years after dad moved to Australia.

I had just finished working at Nestledunn, where I slaved in a factory making mattresses for barely any pay, and was on my way home. I had this tatty-looking black mountain bike that was garnished with rust—rough to the touch and if you used the brakes you could literally hear the bike scream. So there I was, brother, riding back to my shoebox flat on the outskirts of the city centre when all of a sudden, BAM! A hellish mixture of screams from passers-by, breaking glass and metal on metal confrontation filled the air around me. I lay on my back, my heart pounding like it wanted to burst free from my chest and seek revenge, oblivious to feeling any pain due to an emergency prescription of adrenaline and shock. A few faces gathered round, blurrily asking muffled questions. I let the lack of blood on the car console me after I saw the dents—I was bearing in mind what you used to say about silver linings, brother! The sirens of the ambulance wailed on the horizon, the rush hour traffic not helping my cause. From all this chaos and confusion came forth a heavenly creature. I could see her face as clear as a crystal and infinitely more beautiful, amid the blurred gaggle of helpful strangers. She knelt next to my shoulder, brushed her auburn hair from her face and with the same hand gently stroked my forehead. A tear rolled down her cheek. 'I'm so sorry,' she said shakily. I looked at her sorrowful visage, raised the best smile I could and replied, 'Don't you worry yourself, beautiful. Everything's gonna be alright. You hear me?' She smiled.

A broken leg in plaster and a few hours later I got an unexpected visitor at the hospital. Rosaleen. She had been a wreck from guilt and had to see how I was. Bless her. We chatted for what seemed like an eternity. She held my hand; I stroked hers with my thumb. I told her she could leave and she had nothing to worry about. I guess I was just testing to see if she'd stay. She said her farewell and kissed my forehead before turning to leave. 'Rosaleen ...' She turned and pinned me down with her gaze. 'Do you want to get a drink sometime? With me?'

Our first date was unique and intense, brother. Having my leg in plaster put a limit on what we could actually do but it was quite an ice-breaker. We ended up having a quiet drink and a 'stroll' by the river. I've never been able to open up like that with someone so soon before. I told her everything. I told her about you, about mum and how dad left. She told me about her family. It was funny looking back on it. On one hand there was me missing dad and on the other there was Rosaleen wanting freedom from hers. It seemed like we represented what the other wanted in life. Only, I didn't know her father back then.

Oh, shit. I'm gonna be sore soon. Only fell asleep up on the roof last night, didn't I? Got bloody woken up by the sun painting my face pink. Jesus, it's hot today. Too hot to be travelling, that's for sure. Sorry, brother, you're gonna have to wait another day, I'm not going anywhere. It's a nice enough spot, with the friendly rustling of the trees on the other side of the canal. They may have overtaken the footpath, but in return they offer shade when needed—a gesture of natural kindness. I wouldn't mind sharing a day like this with someone, to be honest. Anyone. Strange thing is, Nevan, I've had times when I've chatted to people, people I've not seen before, and little mannerisms of theirs take me back to Ireland. Whether it's a lady brushing the hair from her face as she walks with her dog along the towpath, or seeing the look of relief on a labourer's face as he enters the pub, I get a familiar feeling. At first my heart skips a beat and I have to take a second glance, then that feeling of loss creeps in. I'm not happy with it, brother: a polite conversation with a stranger can end with me having to say goodbye to Rosaleen or dad again.

I couldn't quite tell if the shower was stinging my face or if it was soothing it. Do you remember Cornwall, brother? Our first family holiday in England and we got burnt to hell on the second day. I remember dad saying, 'Don't worry, it's nothing a cold shower won't fix!' Well I don't know if it actually helps but I'm still doing it to this day. He was a good man to us when we were little ones, wasn't he? I remember the time we had the slightest snow. As soon as he heard us get excited he disappeared to the garage to build us a sledge. I can't imagine Rosaleen's dad ever being like that at all. To be fair, though, he had me fooled long enough.

Things were going really well with Rosaleen. It was your classic whirlwind romance. We had been going out for about a year when I lost my job at Nestledunn. I didn't let it get me down, though, I looked for the silver lining. I saw the whole situation as a chance to make a fresh start with Rosaleen. My redundancy pay was enough to cover my rent while I tried to get a job that she'd be proud of me for. It was a sign.

I didn't have much luck finding work. I remember the mild disdain that contaminated the faces of potential employers when they saw that my credentials consisted of a handful of O-Levels and a couple of years work experience in a factory. Rosaleen was due to finish university and move into my flat, which didn't help alleviate any pressure off me finding a job. But it all took a turn one afternoon when Rosaleen told me she had spoken to her father. Donal Fiontan. I hadn't had the chance of meeting him yet and she hadn't told me much about him either, other than he was very controlling. Apparently, it was Donal who decided she was going to be a teacher and where she was going to study to do so. He said she could do whatever she wanted at university and study wherever she wanted; but if she wanted his help financially she had to do things on his terms. Rosaleen said he had an opening down at his nightclub. Nothing fancy, just doing the odd job during the day and bar work at night, but it was something.

Meeting Donal for the first time was quite something. I anticipated it being awkward, meeting the future father-in-law for the first time, but instead it was very business-like. We met in the club of his where I was to be working, White Fire, a sprawling construction that looked as though it was clad in silver armour. I arrived a bit early and was greeted by Terry, the bar manager. Terry got me a drink and told me a bit about the club: how long it had been open under their management, how they turned the club around from when they bought it and the origin of the name. The big, icy steel door opened and Donal entered with the smoothness and ferocity of an arctic breeze, accompanied by his crow-like assistant flapping by his side. Donal didn't look me up and down at all, even though this was the first time we had met. His eyes were constantly locked onto mine like he had more interest in my soul than my flesh. 'Joseph Conall?' was all he greeted me with. Everything about this man was cold, brother: the blue-grey eyes, precise handshake, grey hair and matching suit. He didn't once mention Rosaleen, even to ask if she was alright. It made me think that Rosaleen didn't tell him I was her boyfriend, but she assured me she did—she said it was another example of him being emotionally neglectful. I should've taken the frosty atmosphere as a sign not to work there. Things could have been so different.

Canal life can be deceptive at times, brother. When I bought my narrow boat, it must have been, what ... 2003? I imagined the 'on the road' lifestyle, only on water. Sleep in a different place every night to fully enjoy getting my freedom back. That seems like a joke now because, at the end of the day, no matter how different it looks outside of the window I'm still confined to the same little space. Feels like another cell, only on water. No point paying any tax either, I remember thinking, I'll just save my money and keep moving. Ha! It wasn't long before I got caught out. My boat definitely isn't designed for speedy getaways. It just means you can't really make many long lasting friendships—everyone literally just passes by one another, smiling.

I had a terrible nightmare the other night. I was in my cell back in Castlerea, lying on my bunk, and I had a visit from Donal. He told me they would never free me as long as he was alive. He left, then my cell started to rock and sway as if it were on stormy waters. I could hear the ceaseless pecking of the rain on the roof and walls, as if my cell were a stand-alone building. The rain got louder and louder till I woke and realised that the sound of ducks nibbling the side of the boat had blended into my dream. It's been a long time since I had a prison dream but not long enough, brother. I'll never forgive Donal for what he's done to me. Three years he took. Three years and everything else.

Things were going really well since working at White Fire. I wasn't earning much but it was a significant amount more than I was getting from Nestledunn and the work was much more bearable. Me and Rosaleen were getting on better than ever, despite me teasing her about her surname meaning white fire. It wasn't long before we got engaged and were making some serious plans for our future. Working at the club it was interesting to get to watch people letting their hair down and celebrating for no reason other than it not being daytime anymore. After a couple of weeks faces began to stick and there was no longer a cloud of strangers. Now there was the same group of lads as last week, trying it on with the same group of girls that rejected them the week before. Only they were too drunk to remember and the cycle continued to the next week. Working in a club you also learn to spot the signs that'll tell you if someone's drunk or on drugs. It wasn't long before I noticed some of the regular faces selling ecstasy pills and cocaine on the sly, and it looked like they were making a small fortune in the process. Well, brother, you know how we were brought up: our parents were Beatles fans not Elvis fans. So I rang the police, they took their action and the little drug operation was no more. Unfortunately for me, I was unaware that the faces selling drugs were also under the secret employ of Donal Fiontan. Not being able to shift lost him a lot of tax-free income and he wasn't happy. Surprisingly, he kept me on working nights as a barman, although I could tell he didn't really want me there. Then a month or so after the drug scandal, what I thought was another business disaster happened to Donal: there was an armed robbery shortly after the club had closed for the night.

I was sentenced to three years in a medium security prison, Castlerea. Forgive me if I don't mention what they convicted me for, brother—I don't believe in saying I got convicted for something I didn't do. That bastard Donal implicated me to the police, and made sure I got sent down. When I was released he was waiting for me in his black 4x4, complete with tinted windows. The crow got out and ushered me in. For a moment as I sat there, the car filled with a sinister leathery smell, the thought entered my head that they were going to kill me. Donal told me he had intercepted my letters to Rosaleen. He also said that there was no point trying to contact her as she was pregnant and had moved on, and that I was dead to her. He pulled out a photo of her from his wallet. She looked as beautiful with her baby bump as I had always imagined she would. She looked happy. I felt my heart sink and my stomach churn.

I arrived in England later that night and drank for a few days. Donal had given me a several thousand pounds, presumably so I kept my mouth shut and left him in control, and told me to go to England and never come back. I bought the boat with the money Donal gave me off a Dutch immigrant who was desperate to sell. I hope you don't find me buying a narrow boat in bad taste, brother; it just reminded me of my first date with Rosaleen down by the river. Anyway, I renamed her in your honour. The 'Let It Be,' she's called. I remember lying out in the garden at summertime, and you kept getting mum to play it again and again. By the end of the summer she was sick of her favourite song.

There it is, Nevan, there's the bridge; and that's the lock. It's eerily quiet, no birdsong in my ears tonight. The sky looks like a demonstration of grey scale, while the air hangs dense and melancholy. I'll moor up before I come to the lock, brother. So, will mum be with you? How's her chest? I haven't heard from dad in over six years, is he with you too? I've been thinking about this day for some time now, I can't believe it's finally here. I can sense you around me, brother, sounds crazy I know. What was that sound? Sounded like static from a radio, someone's probably got one outside. I've often thought about which way I should go when I get here: a massive overdose, jumping from a height or slitting my wrists.

Seventeen years ago you left us, Nevan. I remember it vividly. Seeing you fall into the lock and disappear under the boat. Consumed by water and sealed under by a narrow boat. It's a moment seared into my memory. As I pull the knife from the kitchenette draw, a warped reflection of my face stares back from the blade. I temporarily glaze over. Thoughts of Irish fields, happy families and Rosaleen wash through my mind until something else weans into my conscious.

Whisper words of wisdom, let it be.

Let it be? That radio hasn't worked in a long while; brother, are you playing tricks on me? Am I crazy? Maybe I should put the knife away. Now what do I do? I could sell the boat and try and make another fresh start. Or I could try and find Rosaleen. A good night's sleep should bring some answers. And I'll see what dreams await.

Guy Kelly was born 5 years later to the day Elvis died (16 August 1982) in Gravesend (burial place of Pocahontas), Kent. Shortly before turning 18 he moved to Rochester (once home to Charles Dickens) before leaving for university in Winchester (once home to Jane Austen) in 2000. Guy is currently in his third year studying Creative Writing, and Media and Film Studies.

AMBROSIA

BRENDA G. WOOLEY

It is late fall, and we are on our way to have Sunday dinner with my maternal great-grandparents. We have been there before, but I am eight years old and this is the visit I will remember.

My older brother, Johnny, my younger sister, Libby, and I sit in the back seat of the Nash as we enter Beech Grove, turning at Judge Wilson's mammoth three-story house with gingerbread trim, driving past Cordelia O'Shea's tiny cottage where we were once invited in to see her parakeet, and on down Mulberry Street to the corner of Chinaberry, where Papa eases the big car up to the curb.

The old house sits high on a hill overlooking the street, the bare branches of the giant oaks standing guard. At one end of the long front porch a swing rattles in the cold wind; at the opposite end are two silent rocking chairs, their matching cushions caved in, as if two invisible people keep watch. Dry, parched leaves, rustling like tissue paper, flit across the yard.

We tumble out of the Nash and scramble up the steep embankment to the pathway but stop dead still when our great-grandmother appears at the door. She looks as fragile as the leaves, this person from another time. Her hair, still black but for a few threads of grey, is gathered in a roll at the nape of her neck, and the white lace collar of her dark dress flutters in the gathering wind as her sunken eyes give us a dark and piercing look.

We take a step backward when our great-grandfather materializes behind her. He is dressed in a brown suit and vest, a gold watch-chain dangling from the breast pocket. His head is edged in a fringe of snow-white hair, a few strands combed carefully across the dome. A sudden gust of wind picks them up and waves them back and forth as Momma and Papa catch up with us. In a flurry of greetings, we are moved inside.

The parlor is dark and foreign. A huge brown horsehair sofa sits along one wall faced by two matching chairs, their backs draped with large crocheted doilies. A mahogany library table sits between the chairs, and an enormous grandfather clock ticks in the corner. Mouthwatering aromas drift from the kitchen, so we head in that direction.

'Ya'll come on back here, now,' Papa says, motioning to the couch. 'Sit down.'

He removes his hat and places it on the library table as Grampy grabs the arms of his chair, his arms trembling as he lowers his body into a sitting position. Papa sits down in the chair opposite him, and we arrange ourselves in a line on the sofa.

Momma follows Granny into the dining room, the door swinging shut behind them, and all is quiet except the ticking of the grandfather clock. Every time I move, the horsehair scratches my legs, but I can't seem to sit still.

Grampy lifts one foot and strikes a match on the sole of his shoe, cupping his shaky hands around the flame as he sticks it into the bowl of his pipe. Puffs of vanilla-scented smoke spout upward as his wrinkled cheeks sink in and poof out. He settles back in his chair and crosses his legs, smoke swirling around his face.

'Well, John, I hear they're gonna build a big nuclear plant up there around Paducah.'

'Yep,' Papa says. 'They say they'll put about a thousand men to work when it's up and running.'

Johnny, making sure he is not being noticed, rises and saunters into the bedroom. Libby and I follow.

The room is cold and dark, heavy with the scent of mothballs. A large cannon-ball bed, covered with a white crocheted spread, sits against one wall. I imagine my great-grandparents in it at night, asleep in the darkness, and I shiver. A matching dresser crouches on clawed feet against the opposite wall. The oval mirror is tilted, and our small pale faces seem out of place in this strange, dark place.

Our attention is drawn to a portrait of a man hanging over the bed. I have been told he is our great-great uncle Fred, Granny's brother. He has thick white hair and a long beard, and his eyes glare at us as though he knows we are snooping. He scares us out of the bedroom and back into the living room.

'I read in the paper that everything was quiet,' Papa is saying, 'and all of a sudden somebody in the back of the room yelled, "Give 'em hell, Harry!"'

'Hee, hee, hee,' Grampy says, 'that Truman's really something.'

We burst through the dining room door and almost collide with Granny, who is carrying a sweet potato casserole.

'Y'all need to go on outside,' she says in her hoarse voice.

My mouth waters as I watch the melting marshmallows trickle down the inside of the glass dish.

'You children need fresh air. Y'all look peaked.'

Johnny and Libby return to the parlor, and I examine my face in the mirrored back of the china cabinet. *What does peaked mean, anyway?*

Granny returns to the kitchen, and I tiptoe to the enormous cherry dining table which is set for dinner. The delicate china plates are sprinkled with tiny lilacs, and the crystal glasses look as though they would shatter if I touched them. The silverware gleams, and I cannot resist picking up a knife. It is much heavier than our knives at home, and they all match. There are white cloth napkins, and I wonder why, since all anyone does with them is wipe off their mouths. I imagine Granny at the old wringer washer on the back porch, dousing them with 'bluing,' running them through the wringer, hanging them on the clothesline, bringing them inside, sprinkling them, rolling them up, and sweating through the back of her dress as she leans over the ironing board, sliding a heavy black iron back and forth.

A sudden flash of light draws my attention to a large cut-glass bowl in the center of the dining table. It is most beautiful thing I have ever seen. The noonday sun slices through the brilliant glass, casting tiny diamond-shaped sparkles along the opposite wall, and I move closer where I can see each cut in the delicate glass. The longer I gaze it, the more it seems to shimmer and glitter with a life of its own.

'Didn't we tell y'all to go outside,' Granny says, as she enters the dining room. She is carrying a large platter of roast beef, surrounded by tiny butter-glazed potatoes.

As I am searching for an answer, Momma comes in. She and Granny begin talking and moving dishes around on the table, so I slink to the kitchen door and push it open.

A large roaster sits on the stove, the juices still simmering. A bunch of bananas and oranges lie on the surface of the cabinet in the corner. There is also a big coconut. I have never seen a coconut except in stores, since Momma always buys it in a can. I creep across the kitchen and lightly touch its hairy shell. It seems foreign, like the bedroom, the cloth napkins on the dining table, the scratchy furniture in the living room, and Granny and Grampy themselves.

As I head back down the hall to the dining room, I gaze up at a big, old-fashioned portrait on the wall. A solemn-faced couple, whom I have been told is Granny and Grampy on their wedding day, gaze down at me. Grampy, with a mustache, his thick, dark hair parted in the middle, sits unsmiling in an old-fashioned suit. Granny stands beside him, her long tapered fingers resting on his shoulder. She is wearing a long dress with a bustle, a brooch pinned at the high-collared neck. Their faces seem carved in stone. It is hard to believe these two unwrinkled, straight-backed people are my ancient great-grandparents. I know they are the same people, but I feel there is more to it.

The dining room door opens and Granny enters. She appears not to see me, so I freeze, as she carefully pours a mixture of oranges, bananas and coconut into the exquisite cut-glass bowl. Before returning to the kitchen, she turns to me.

'That is ambrosia,' she says, 'and this bowl is only for ambrosia.'

Her dark eyes are stern, and she continues to stare at me, so I nod.

I hurry back into the living room, which is now empty, and sit down on the scratchy sofa. The clock is still ticking, the room shadowy, and even though no one else is there, the room seems occupied.

Johnny and Libby burst through the door, their cheeks rosy, and Papa and Grampy follow. Soon it is time for dinner.

Though no one tells us to be quiet, we don't say a word during the meal. The adults discuss various people they know who went to Detroit to get jobs and are now planning to come back to this area when the big nuclear plant is built.

'Arnold Titsworth told me he'll be back here quicker than you can skin a cat,' Grampy says, laughing.

'Well, I don't blame him for wanting to come back home,' Papa says, 'Things are really booming in Western Kentucky.'

Finally, it is time for dessert, and I can hardly wait to taste the ambrosia in the glittering bowl.

It seems an eternity before Granny passes my bowl to me. I pick up my heavy silver spoon and dip it into the luscious fruit, being careful not to drip juice on the white tablecloth. I plunk the fruit into my mouth and immediately feel as though I am going to throw up. Right there on the spotless tablecloth.

It tastes like nothing I have ever tasted in my life. I love bananas, oranges and coconut, but the combination is just too much. I hold the mixture in my mouth, looking around for a place to get rid of it, but there is nothing to do but sit there and hold it in my mouth. Everyone else seems to be enjoying it. Finally, I swallow it, and then I put my spoon down and sit in silence.

When dinner is over, Papa and Grampy go back into the living room, and Johnny and Libby go outside. Momma carries dishes into the kitchen, and Granny begins gathering up the bowls.

As I am getting up from the table, Granny turns and places one blue-veined hand on my shoulder. 'You didn't eat your ambrosia.'

I don't know what to say, so I nod.

'I must admit, I didn't much like ambrosia when I was your age either.' An impish smile slips over her face, and I glimpse, just for an instant, the young bride in the wedding picture. 'The bowl is magnificent, though. My grandmother gave it to me,' she says, picking up the glittering bowl, 'and she told me I would someday pass it down to my own daughter or granddaughter. But I never did. It seemed none of them appreciated its beauty as much as I did.' She looks at me and smiles. 'But you do, don't you?' She gazes out the window where the setting sun picks up the gold in her brown eyes. 'I couldn't imagine getting old like my grandmother,' she says, 'but here I am.'

It is thus that I will remember her, preserved in this immortal moment of a late Sunday afternoon, the glow of the autumn sun illuminating the planes in her face, the gold in her eyes, the hint of the bride she once was.

I am in my first semester at college when Momma calls to tell me Granny has passed away. 'I don't think she ever recovered from Grampy's death,' Momma says. 'She just gave up.'

As I enter Beech Grove, the Corvair, as though it has a mind of its own, turns at Judge Wilson's house with the gingerbread trim, past Cordelia O'Shea's cottage, which is boarded up now, then on down Mulberry to the corner of Chinaberry.

Snow covers the ground, and the old house seems smaller than I remember. The rocking chairs are gone, and the porch looks bare. The swing is still.

The old grandfather clock ticks in the living room, and the horsehair sofa and chairs are in the same places. They now seem quaint and appealing. I hear the scratch of a match near Grampy's chair, and the faint scent of vanilla drifts through the air.

The big cannon-ball bed still holds court, the smell of mothballs lingers, and from his portrait above the bed, Uncle Fred's eyes follow me. The room seems to sigh.

The dining room table is laden with cakes and casseroles that neighbors always bring by when there is a death in the family. The mammoth oak cabinet stands in the shadows, the delicate china and thin crystal still in the same places. The ambrosia bowl is there on the shelf, dusty now.

The kitchen is cold, but Granny's steps echo there on the worn spots in the linoleum in front of the stove and sink. On the counter I see the oranges, bananas, and the big coconut. And I see myself, the ghost of my childhood.

I look at the old house once more as I start up the Corvair, and then I leave the fading photographs, the treasured possessions, the memories, the dying shadows of another age, and drive on down the winding streets toward the funeral home.

I am a grandmother now, and when I pass a mirror I often fail to recognize myself. Who is that woman, the one with grey hair and lines in her face? And then I remove the ambrosia bowl from my china cabinet and walk to the window, holding it to the light. I am there again, seeing it as I saw it then ... shimmering and glittering, tiny diamond-shaped sparkles bouncing along the opposite wall, gazing off into the distance as the setting sun casts a soft glow across Granny's face. And mine.

Brenda G. Wooley's work has appeared in *Southern Hum, River Walk Journal, Amarillo Bay, Arabesques Review* and elsewhere. She has lived in Illinois and Michigan and now makes her home near Paducah, Kentucky, where she is at work on her novel, *Journey to a Normal Life.*

SUBWAY STORY

MIKE AMATO

He liked words like *jewel* and *luminary*—words that pursed the lips when spoken. And names like *Lillian* and *Juliet*. 'It should be pronounced with only two syllables,' he declared once in class. 'If you follow the meter, you see that her name must be pronounced "Ju-lyet."' He then demonstrated, proudly proclaiming with curled lips, 'It *is* the *East* and *Ju*-liet *is* the *sun*!' The '-liet' was the best part of the word. It sounded like a ripple in the ocean, or a small bird alighting on a spray.

These were among the top twenty on a list of words that he had recorded over the years in his spiral notebook, which he carried tucked under his arm as he left his Lower East Side apartment building. These were the words and names that were bound to be included in his first story, the first chronicle of his life in New York.

The plan was to take the subway up to Central Park, to Strawberry Fields, lie down on the grass and there let it happen. He was nearly equipped: gray slacks for self-assurance, a green shirt for inspiration, seven bucks for lunch and a Metrocard for the subway.

But first he had to stop at the drugstore to get a new pen.

His wingtips made a sound on the store's linoleum that was different than the sound they made on the pavement—more of a *clacking* than a *clocking*. At the register, he found the perfect ballpoint pen, which he decided to break in then and there on the counter itself. The dowdy, middle-aged clerk, holding a peeled tangerine in her yellowed fingers, placidly watched him scratch a few tiny laps with the implement over countless ink swirls that were already scribbled on the countertop.

'One-twenty-five,' she muttered, as she sucked another segment of citrus from her fingers. She made masticating noises with the bits of tangerine in her mouth as she took the money, a guttural gurge as she extracted juices from the fruit and rang up the merchandise.

Putting the auditory ugliness behind him, he strode down Delancey Street toward the Grand Street station. As he clacked along he could feel a rumble beneath his feet, like something burrowing below the hot pavement, and he quickened his pace.

It was common to feel that volcanic stir at strange moments throughout the city—while watching a movie at the Angelika, or lunching at Dojo's. To some it was simply the mechanics of a metropolis, but to him it was the baseline to the music of the city. Much of what he'd written over the years, mostly paragraphs and fragments, was about the subway. The 'steel mole,' he called it.

He rounded the corner and raced down the stairs of the station, his notebook in one hand and his Metrocard in the other. He passed through the turnstile and felt the dust and the distant rumble of the express train settle onto the quiet subway platform. He walked around in circles listening to his heels clacking on the craggy concrete floor as the noise bounced off the wall's white tiles. On the other side of the station, the downtown side, a Japanese musician began scratching his strange violin. Then, there was a slight change in the air pressure, and he closed his eyes and anxiously listened. A low, distant tremor was born, followed by a blast of the mole's hot breath. He looked down the tunnel as the tremor grew into a gurgling rumble. The walls of the shaft began to glow, the clamor rising to a roar, until from the arching cave showed the eyes of the screaming metal beast. As it rushed past his face, the wind and ruckus washed over him like a tidal wave. It whipped him with air until it slowly stumbled to a halt and opened its silver portals to him.

He'd been on the Metro in D.C. and the Underground in London, but nothing compared to the ferocity of the New York City subway. Nothing stirred him like the churning of the mole, and nothing felt more familial to him. After all, his blood was in the very veins of the city.

His great-grandfather was one of hundreds of Italian immigrants who built the first subway tunnels from City Hall to 145th Street. He had moved the family from Palermo to the Lower East Side, where his sons and grandsons grew up to maintain the tunnels, and where, a century later, his great-grandson now lived, nested in a brick-red tenement along with his bed and laptop.

And Juliet. Or so he had renamed her. He couldn't abide the name 'Julie,' but Juliet ... Nor could he abide the muffled, cracking noise she made when she ate a hard pretzel with her mouth closed. That muted report drummed up the very primal fears in him—the breaking of bones beneath the skin, one animal devouring another. In most things to do with sounds, he preferred *legato* to *staccato*.

For her part, Julie was surprisingly supportive of her new moniker, knowing that she couldn't compare with a Lillian or a Michelle.

'*Michelle*,' he said aloud. The uptown B train thrashed him back and forth in his seat as he surrendered himself to the whims of the car and flipped open his notebook. 'A perfectly fluid name,' he thought as he rearranged the words on his list. He closed his eyes and whispered it once again. He then recorded the corresponding sound next to the name: '—a kiss followed by a sigh.'

He closed his notebook and let his eyes wander the train until he finally let them come to rest on the chest of a young Nubian woman. He carelessly held his stare warmly on her bosom, which was nestled in a tight black shirt wrapped in a cool leather coat. For a moment his line of sight collided with hers and they both darted away uncomfortably, but his gaze slowly drifted back only to spy the gold chain around her neck, the name on which sat askew on her right breast. The angle at which her chest supported the necklace made it impossible to read from his vantage; but, with a slight jostle from his friend the mole, the necklace shifted in his favor, crawling down her breast and presenting itself proudly over her cleavage. He squinted to see. What he imagined to be a name actually turned out to be a shape. A shape of what? Careful glancing finally revealed the image. It was a lamb. Yes, definitely a lamb.

He perused the woman: short hair, slick fingers firmly gripping a black bag on her lap. This was no lamb, he thought. But she was no wolf, either.

The West 4th station flashed by the windows and the train jerked and jumped its way to a gradual stop. As the young woman stood up and moved toward the door, a thick, pale, sallow-haired man in a dirty red sweatshirt and matching pants plopped himself down into her place. He slowly nestled in, allowing himself to overflow into the adjacent occupied seats. The man stared blankly for a while as his neighbors shifted and scootched in order to accommodate him. Snapping out of his stare, he plunged into a white deli bag that rested on his gut, pulling out chunks of white cheese from a calzone. The man alternately fed from his deli bag and his bag of potato chips, liberally dumping crumbs onto his red sweatshirt and the floor around him. He paused periodically to glance around with a guilty expression, his gray-stubbled cheeks filled with his slop, before returning to his meal.

This was worse than the tangerine lady, he thought, and he pulled away from the sight with a visible look of disgust. Having had his fill of the sweaty man, he tucked his new pen into his shirt pocket and proceeded to the next stomach of the mole through the front of the car.

Outside, the mole was screaming, inside, its voice was reduced to a muted wail. He danced his way over to a seat opposite two middle-aged working men, one a small, salt-and-peppered black fellow in a white T-shirt and black trousers, the other a rough, dumpy Mexican in a gray windbreaker. Both had the blissful haze of early-morning intoxication. The old black fellow chattered on vigorously two-and-a-half inches from the chubby face of his friend who sat smiling and nodding like an evangelical on lithium. He listened carefully to the man over the din of the car, but all he could make out was a distorted yet deliberate chicken-babble. It didn't dispirit the Mexican, however, who pretended to understand exactly what his friend was saying.

'Cuz you ga-go go yio do no good no go choon do, man!'

The old Mexican quietly agreed, nodding, smiling, as the other shook his head with a titter. The Mexican mimicked his friend's wonder with a shaking of his own head. His smile occasionally turned away before it was called back by another purposeful rant. Each rant, from what he could discern, seemed to say exactly the same thing. After a while, he realized that the babble he was hearing was the Spanish language.

Suddenly, in the middle of a joyful dissertation, the old man stood up and demonstrated to his friend a glorious little jig. 'De-de-de-de-de!' he sang as he shuffled back and forth for a moment, then returned to his seat and laughed into his friend's face. The smiling Mexican nodded his appreciation while the rest of the passengers, save he, ignored the event. The old man repeated his rant to his friend, stood up to re-enact his dance with a 'De-de-de-de-de!' then returned to his friend's face to get his smiling recognition.

To the left of the dancing man sat a fat, curly-haired man in shorts and blue T-shirt. His thick, curly mop—his 'Euro,' perhaps—supported a yellow cap perched atop which, along with his reddish hair and blue T-shirt, completed a bold primary-color ensemble. He held a small tape recorder to the side of his head and grinned wide-eyed and dull-witted at what he was listening to.

This exotic spectacle intrigued the old black man, who turned to his left and looked up his brow at the curly-haired man next to him with a misty, drunken smirk. The curly-haired man, uncomfortably aware of the old man's scrutiny, strained to maintain his air of aplomb by looking straight ahead, his huge noggin soaking up the vibrations from his pocket radio. The man's nervous eyes buckled once or twice under the pressure of his examination, which resulted in strange smiles from the both of them.

The train arrived at the 72nd street station on the West Side of the park just before 9 a.m. As he climbed up the station stairs, the sun came over the buildings and stabbed him in the eyes. He turned to the park and drank in the panorama—people walking every kind of dog, tourists, hotdog vendors, strollers, buses, rollerbladers. He stepped into Strawberry Fields amidst the American elm and willow trees and decided to walk the path that the sun created for him, past the wilted ceremonial flowers, past the dazed New Yorkers, past a scrawny man in a yogi headstand. He moved to the highest point of the narrow field and took off his shirt. He settled down on the grass, removed his shoes and socks, and lay back slowly, with pageantry and ceremony on his mind, for this was a great occasion. He was finally going to embrace, or become embraced by, that babbling stream of divinity. He got out his little blue spiral notebook and set it by his side before lowering himself completely.

He didn't feel anything yet. He just lay back in the sun, combing his fingers through his hair several times. A minute went by and each blade of grass in its turn stung his sweaty back. The sun began to sear. Little lumps on the ground emerged beneath him, nudging him in the wrong places. After a quarter of an hour, he had had enough.

On his way out of the park, he took his new pen out of his pocket. As he walked past a storm drain, he dropped it through the grate, where it landed on a hill of identical pens.

On the train ride home he felt almost dead. Almost. 'That agonizing word,' he thought. He'd been in the state of 'almost' all his life, it seemed. That tickling, unbearable state—like standing in water up to your eyelids.

As the great metal beast carried him home to his Juliet, he felt an agonizing gnaw at the nape of his neck. The faces of the afternoon travelers seemed darker, taking on a purple hue in his cogitative eye.

He didn't go home. In fact, he rode the train all the way out to Coney Island. He stayed on the train as it sat at the station. He then rode it back and changed to the F which, after an hour, brought him out to Jamaica, Queens, where it sat for a spell. From there, the train pulled him back to the shuttle to LaGuardia Airport. He then got on the E, changed to the A, and rode it all the way out to Far Rockaway. This went on for several more hours, and he never left the subway—not at the Bronx Zoo, not at the Battery, not at the Brooklyn Navy Yard—until he arrived back at Delancey Street some time in the wee morning hours of the next day.

As he emerged from the Delancy Street station, he heard the steel mole screaming away beneath him. In front of him stood the Williamsburg Bridge bickering with its neighbor, the Manhattan Bridge, while the Brooklyn Bridge simply stayed out of the whole affair. His stomach snarled at him, so he took three dollars out of his pocket, stepped into a shop and bought himself a calzone.

Mike Amato works as a writer and actor in New York City. He has a BA in Drama from Marywood University. As both an actor and a comedian, he has toured the United States, performed at Caroline's on Broadway in NYC and has appeared on the legendary U.S. television show Saturday Night Live.

Compositions

Gary Haigh

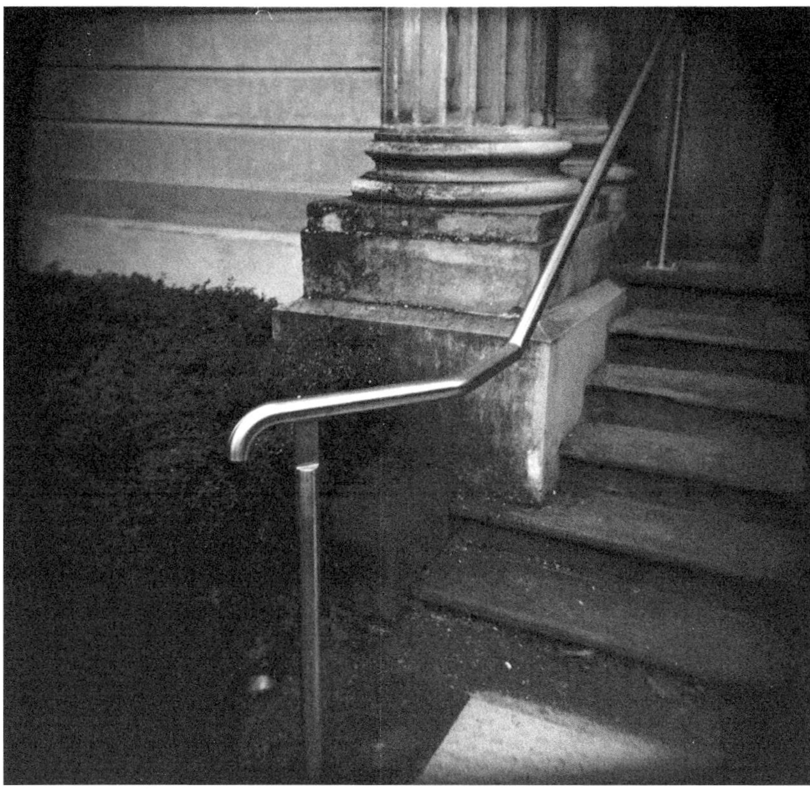

Gary Haigh is an Adelaide photographer who has most recently exhibited at the Leica Gallery, Melbourne. He has a long and loving involvement with light. He draws inspiration from many sources, including the words of the Zenrin and the compositions of Takemitsu and Satie. The images reproduced here are an attempt to draw attention to objects and places sometimes considered banal. They were taken with a 6x6 medium format camera, with the negatives scanned into Adobe Photoshop and then digitally enhanced.

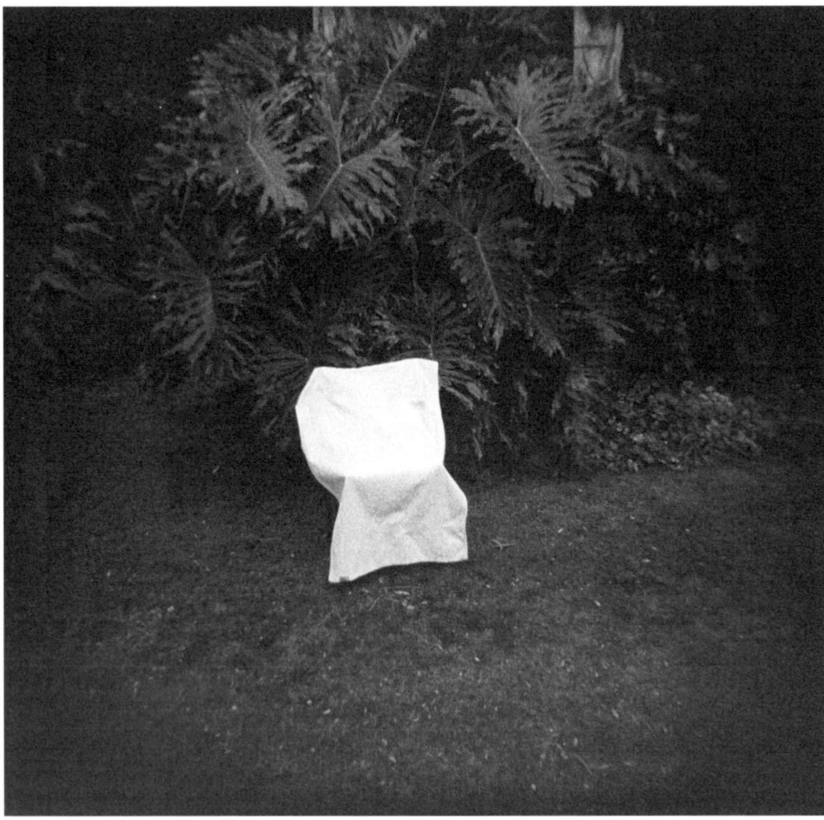

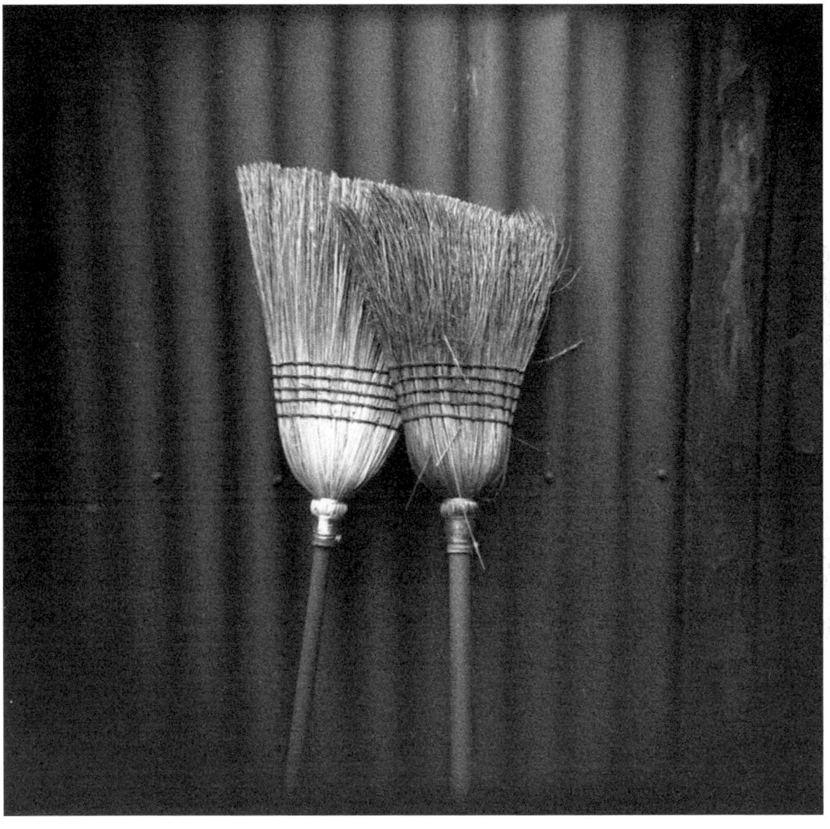

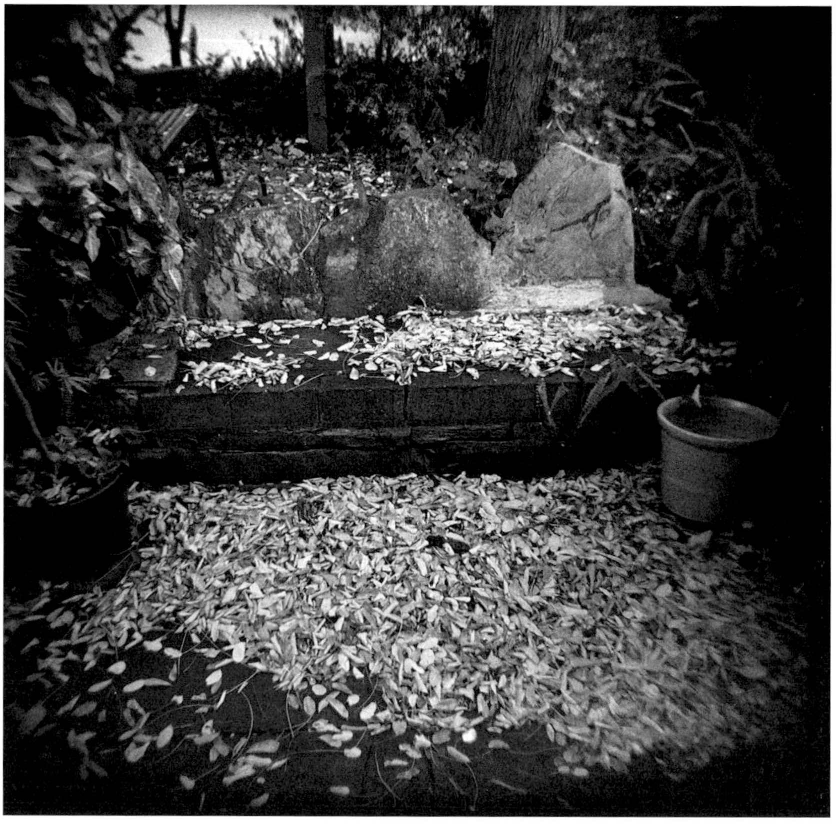

Dark Man Walking

Extract from a Novel

Tony Bugeja

The First Morning

04.15 a.m. Leon awoke in darkness. He switched on the bedside radio, listened to the international news for a few minutes, and went back to sleep. A plane had crashed into a New York tower, but America was a long way from Lacuna. Outside his window, magpies rehearsed their morning calls in a low key and a cat strolled silently home.

07.03 a.m. The taxi driver watched as Tina Finch limped out of the main entrance of the City Hospital and approached his cab. She wore a coat, a headscarf, and another piece of cloth wrapped around the neck and across her lower face. The driver did consider such a thorough covering peculiar; the morning was not especially cold, but he thought the woman may have been hiding some sort of accident or surgical wound. People left hospitals in all sorts of states and some of them got into his taxi. The driver's view was confirmed when he saw that she carried a large paper carrier bag with a pharmacy docket stapled to it.

'Where to?'

'Lacuna, please, Federation Street.'

The driver started the meter, and—as someone who prided himself on being able to start a conversation—said, 'You look like you've got half the chemist shop there.'

Tina did not reply. The driver found a gap in the traffic and drove the cab to Lacuna without saying another word. He assumed that she could not speak English even though she had given directions a few seconds before.

As people do after a period away, Tina looked out of the car window for changes to familiar territory. The park was the same; the magpies and galahs had moved but that was to be expected. The traffic lights still went through their familiar sequence from green to amber and then red.

It was while waiting for the lights to change that Tina noticed a yellow van parked on the verge. On the side of the vehicle in large black letters were the words: 'Nick Cob Fencing Contractor. We Sell Security.' A bald-headed man, holding a mobile phone in one hand and a tape rule in the other, leaned against his van and looked towards Lacuna. He noticed Tina watching him and gave a bow. *Funny fellow,* she thought. *Very formal in manner but dressed in a green and yellow tracksuit. Maybe he sleeps in the back of the van.*

The taxi driver briefly wondered if his passenger, with her face covered and carrying a large bag, could be a terrorist. He pushed the idea out of mind but was glad when they reached Lacuna.

07.30 a.m. Joyce stirred at the insistent pawing of the cat on her face. She arose with as much grace as her seventy years would allow, went into the kitchen, fed the feline, put on the kettle, and turned on the radio.

'Jimmy,' said Joyce as she heard the news, 'we are in for a spot of bother.'

Jimmy, her husband, had been in the city cemetery for five years and did not answer. The cat—who thought his name was Jimmy—continued munching from a bowl near the back door. In need of a better response, Joyce stepped into the garden in her dressing gown and loudly addressed the magpies and sparrows.

'War! Arabs!'

The shout by Joyce and the reply of the birds disrupted the mental state of a younger woman meditating in the next garden. Wendy blinked as the outside world invaded her consciousness. She quickly picked up a small heap of pebbles and arranged them into a protective circle in conformity with Wicca rites, perhaps to guard herself from Joyce's voice, perhaps from the scimitar of Islam.

08.17 a.m. A neighbour, on Joyce's side of the street, checked his watch against the car radio. John had already seen the two New York towers collapsing to rubble on television. He wondered if any Arabs were on the payroll at work. John drove out of the driveway and onto the road. He hoped the traffic lights into the city would all be green.

09.00 a.m. Three blocks away from Joyce's house, the Reverend Duncan Donald stood in the kirk of the Lacuna Unreformed Presbyters. He had been preaching the apocalypse for decades; now it had happened, but he didn't have any parishioners to preach to.

Donald had become accustomed to an elderly congregation of about thirty, but last Sunday there had been only nine. The Reverend wondered if his stray flock would return in response to the bad news, but then remembered that some of them were dead. He prayed for the people of New York.

09.13 a.m. At the park end of Federation Street, in the Camille rooming house, the tenants were having their first bowl of cornflakes for the day. Some were eating the cereal in bed, but most had taken their bowls downstairs to the recreation room. They sat and watched the collapsing of the two towers on TV. One individual, Sam, stayed there all day as the television showed five minutes of mayhem in a continuous cycle.

The Placebo Kid

Back in her flat, Tina placed the paper bag on the bathroom vanity shelf while trying to avoid looking in the mirror. She took out the jars and tubes and read the labels while putting them into the medicine cabinet: salicylic acid, propylene glycol, Celestone M, Oilatum, Dimithicream, and dicloxacillan tablets.

Tina walked down the hall past her ex-husband's copy of Bruegel's *Wedding Feast*. The picture reminded her that she had spent ten years with a phoney aesthete who had a medieval view of marriage. Taking part in the medical experiment, and its accompanying $1500, had been a chance for a new start.

Tina had signed the informed consent form handed to her by the CareLab Corporation. The study was to last three months. It was to test an anti-rejection drug. The volunteers took the chemical once and were then to make weekly visits to the lab for two months to give a little blood. A piece of cake!

A couple of weeks after taking the drug a few of the volunteers developed minor rashes or lowered white cell counts, but Tina was fine. It seemed that she had scored the lucky number in the double-blind test. Tina was enviously called the Placebo Kid by the other lab rats.

Then, after six weeks, Tina got a rush of rashes, and a load of lesions. This was big stuff: hands, legs, face, chest, every-bloody-where. Green grow the rashes, oh! Hard little lumps under the skin, like lentils, appeared along the edges of her hands. The CareLab doctor called it pompholyx, as though giving the ailment a name was a cure. Tina started feeling decidedly unwell. The doctor told her to call any time if it got worse. It got worse, but Doctor Pompholyx was not contactable.

Tina went to her GP who sent her immediately to the emergency department of the City Hospital. As she was wheeled off to a ward, Tina's mind was racing with questions. *Did I leave the fridge door open? Did I lock the back door? Did I leave the stove on? Where did I leave my notebook? What do you have to do to get a cigarette in this place?*

As it happened, Tina did not leave the fridge door open, the stove was off, the back door was locked, and the notebook was on the desk. But she did leave some vegetables on the kitchen table.

Tina went into the kitchen and looked at a bunch of spinach decaying on the chopping board. It seemed to sum up the present state of affairs. She lit a cigarette.

The Crusaders

The crusader spirit that awoke in Joyce had difficulty in finding a Saladin. The leafy suburb of Lacuna had a deficiency of Arabs. There had been a Lebanese man who owned the fried chicken shop, but he had disappeared with a blonde counter-assistant to the Gold Coast a year previously. No one considered this to be uniquely Arabic behaviour at the time but, after that morning in September, Joyce remembered the elopement as evidence of Arab lechery.

There was a carpet and rug business in the high street operated by two dark young men. No one thought much of it before the attack on America—such shops are often owned by world travellers with tanned complexions. Joyce, who was not shy about matters of nationality, paid them a call under the pretext of shopping for a rug.

'Are you Arab?'

'No. We are Iranian Armenians.'

'Are you Muslims?'

'No, but we respect Islam. We are Bahá'í.'

Joyce left the shop confused, but convinced of Arab deviousness.

The suburb needed an Arab. Joyce was not the only one who felt the lack. The citizens of Lacuna needed a living three-dimensional person to represent the images of terrorists they almost saw on television.

Leon had an appearance that could have come from anywhere between Gibraltar and Kabul, but Joyce, after the rug shop episode, was less ready to ask her neighbour about his religion.

'Terrible business in New York,' said Joyce at the garden gate.

'Yes,' replied Leon as he scratched the cat behind its ear.

Leon's answer seemed a less than adequate response. Joyce tried again. 'I can't see an ending to it. It's hard to know what to do.'

'It is a time to stay cool. I hope people will not lose their sense of proportion. A perfect world for a terrorist is one where everyone is an extremist.'

A time to stay cool, indeed, thought Joyce. *I never noticed before how dark he is. And there is definitely an accent to his speech.*

She checked the mail box before going indoors. There was a yellow flyer with bold black letters. **'Nick Cob: fencing contractor. We sell security. Get a fence now and pay later.'**

Joyce wasn't sure if she needed a new fence but security seemed a good thing to buy.

Wendy built Wicca circles of pine cones around the herb patch and japonica hedge. Joyce was gaining a reputation as an expert on Arabs; she dropped Leon's name to acquaintances, and told of his casual approach to September 11. John, increasingly stressed about lack of time in his life, spent hours creating a spreadsheet with the purpose of mapping out every minute of his day.

Wendy created a circle of plant pot shards around the water meter, and one made of pieces of quartz around her bed. The quartz proved painful to bare feet and she replaced the stones with gum leaves. John lay awake at night trying to think of ways to save time, and wondering why he was becoming increasingly tired during the day. Lorna, John's partner, lay beside him wondering about his sanity.

Leon first learned that he had become foreign while shopping at the supermarket. He had never been repeatedly short-changed before. When Leon pointed out to the assistant that the correct amount appeared on the screen at the checkout the problem stopped. Then he started to get an unusual proportion of Indonesian and New Zealand coins in the returned money. Leon built up a collection of them in a jar on the possibility of some future overseas trip.

Joyce blossomed. She approached people in the shopping centre and found many with a similar crusader spirit to herself. She stopped talking to Jimmy, and the cat felt neglected. She discovered the joys of the telephone three-way chat and organised a squad of friends with mobile phones to watch the streets for Leon—the phone companies did very well out of Springtime in Lacuna.

Leon became a star with his own loyal paparazzi. People followed him down supermarket aisles—to check that he wasn't poisoning the food. Other concerned citizens peered at Leon in the public library—to see if he was scattering toxic dust into the books. Mothers huddled children to their skirts when he passed by. Leon's shopping bag was a subject of intense curiosity, and noses would press into its interior whenever his back was turned.

Leon's charisma even extended to the clothes he wore. Note was taken of the washing on his Hill's Hoist—in case he was using shirts to signal 'the enemy'—and a couple of pairs of Leon's briefs disappeared from the line without trace.

The Reverend Duncan Donald was dozing in an armchair, with a newspaper on his lap and a cup of cocoa beside him, when the phone rang. In normal circumstances Duncan would have grunted, removed the newspaper, and lumbered across the room, but instead he floated to the phone.

'This is Neighbourhood Watch. There's a window open in your church.'

Without bothering to ask the caller's name, Duncan put on his jacket and floated across the yard from the manse to the kirk. The night seemed blacker than usual. *The street lights are working, but all the brilliance is sucked out of them*. There was the sulphurous smell of rotten eggs in the air. He wandered around the building in search of the offending window, but everything was locked up.

'A nuisance phone call,' muttered the Reverend Donald. 'Probably children. Still, I'd better look inside.' He unlocked the door, dropped his keys, and groped for the light switch.

'Good evening Rev,' said a voice from the dark interior.

'Who are you? There is nothing to steal here.'

'You can say that again,' replied the voice, 'but the real estate is worth a bit.' Duncan flicked the switch and saw a man wearing a green and yellow tracksuit, a mobile phone in one hand and a tape rule in the other, leaning irreverently against the lectern.

'Who the devil are you?'

'Very succinctly put. Look on me as a facilitator from head office.'

'Which head office?'

'Does it matter?'

'Of course it matters. This is a place of worship.'

The man roared with laughter. Everything went black and the Reverend Donald ran out of the kirk with laughter pursuing him. Duncan awoke in his chair. 'I have to get a congregation,' he muttered, 'and I must cut down on the cocoa.'

Sam

Leon was sitting on the bench by the bus stop with his shoulders bent and legs sprawled forward. A jogger approached and he drew his feet in to give her room on the narrow pavement. Leon watched the runner as she passed and ran over a carpet of jacaranda petals.

'That's a soul sucker, grandad,' said a voice to his left.

Leon had not met the speaker before, but he recognised malnutrition. It wasn't the pot-bellied skinny-armed kind of starvation—more of the puffy pale-faced, scratches won't heal, and can't think straight, variety. He had first seen it in Sydney boarding houses decades ago.

Reacting to being called 'grandad,' he retorted, 'My name is Leon. What's yours?'

'Sam.'

He smiled at the name and couldn't resist asking, 'Why do soul-suckers suck-souls, Sam?' He laughed at his own joke.

'You a Leon?' Sam asked, ignoring his question. 'You don't look like a Leon.'

'No, I look like someone who should have an unpronounceable name. That's why it's Leon. What about the soul-suckers?'

'They moved into the cottages and did them up. They sold their souls to do it and run around Lacuna in shorts and joggers hunting for new ones. You were wise to avoid her.'

'Who did they sell their souls to?'

'Some say Satan, but the bank is more likely.'

The bus arrived and Sam strolled down the aisle to the back. Leon found a seat at the front in his place among the elderly and maimed.

The Fencing Contractor

Nick Cob, the fencing contractor, walked from one letterbox to the next distributing fliers. Lacuna was a new start. Soon he planned to have an assistant to do this sort of work. Nick dreamed of a future controlling a network of fencing franchises all around the nation. No more sleeping in the back of a van near the park.

He had picked Lacuna with care. It was a suburb of old money where people took pride in their possessions and feared that politicians, radicals, and newly arrived flat-dwellers had only one aim but to steal them. Each wave of new arrivals, from the Irish to the Vietnamese, had generated a spasm of anxiety. Nick arrived in Lacuna at the right time for a fencing contractor.

Nick had started the business in his home town. Fences and locks were needed but the business did not grow. He knew that the reason for this was that people feared him, although he didn't know the cause. Nick had tried painting a smiley face on the side of the van but it made no difference.

'I'm a nice person,' Nick said to his girlfriend at the time. 'Why don't people like me?'

His girlfriend, who had just returned from seeing the doctor for a sleeping disorder (she did not dream), had no explanation.

When Nick said goodbye to his mother all she had to say was, 'You're a good boy at heart but you've caused me a few sleepless nights.'

Nick did not know that people dreamed about him, and that they dreamt that he was the Devil.

The Pompholyx Diary

Tina Finch sat at her kitchen table and wrote.

> 14/09/2001
> My feet are still sore and the soles are covered in hard lumpy skin. I am forced to wear oversized sneakers with two pairs of socks to get around. Hands are still tender, and peeling, and cut easily. I am using gloves for such tasks as preparing food and washing up. The skin on my legs has settled down a little but the rash erupts when rubbing against rough clothing (e.g. jeans). I am not going to wear joggers—people will think I sleep in them. A long skirt is the only way to go—I'm sorry Germaine

Greer but the body rules. Generally I still tire easily but have improved since leaving hospital.

Tina leaned back on her chair and lit a cigarette. While in hospital she discovered a kind of tobacco underground that bore some resemblance to the freedom railroad. After her first day she would gather with a tribe of smokers in an extreme corner of the grounds. Many of them were homeless men with chronic skin conditions. Tina wasn't sure if their lifestyle created the maladies or if the stigma of the diseases forced the men to the fringes of society. Tina acquired a series of scaly patches along her shins. 'Psoriasis,' said the men with the authority of a choir of dermatologists. 'It comes and goes but lasts for life.'

After four days of drips, pills and lotions, Tina's condition stabilised. A doctor told her that the integrity of her skin had improved. She was also healthy enough for her nomadic ways to become a nuisance around the hospital grounds.

'How long will it take to clear?' asked Tina.

'Impossible to say,' replied the doctor. 'You could stay in this state for many weeks or, one day, it may suddenly clear up for no apparent reason. The skin is less understood than some internal organs.'

Tina was sent home with an array of ointments to treat a condition that could last for months.

15/09/2001

The soles of my feet are cracking, showing open wounds—very dramatic. There may be a limitation on future walking. The top of my head is a mosaic of cracked skin but the face is clearing. I must cover the head but not the face. A scarf—Italian style—with a knot or clasp behind the right ear? A Hijab? No, I don't know how to fold it. An English forties headscarf with the knot at the throat? No, I don't see myself as the fish-wife type. There's a beret in the cupboard. I'll go for a beret and dark glasses. Retro fifties Left Bank; it'll be ok for a couple of weeks. Very existentialist, only I'm not sure if existentialist women wore long skirts. The only quote from Sartre I can remember is 'Hell is other people.'

'To market to market, jiggity-jig,' said Tina to the open fridge. The market in question was Lacuna Supermarket, and the jig was more of a hobble on sore feet.

All was well until Tina went to the checkout. There was a line of six men ahead of her and they were each carrying six packets of cornflakes. It reminded her of a vaguely remembered nursery rhyme about seven wives with seven cats. *Something very odd has happened to Lacuna since I've been away*, she thought.

The checkout worker whisked Tina's items through and took the fifty dollar note, but gave an involuntary shudder when Tina put her scabby hand out for change. *The girl probably thinks it's contagious. She's just a high school student trying to earn a dollar. I shouldn't have put her through this. I'll find some other way to shop.*

19/9/01

My energy level is improved. Psychologically, I am starting to see myself as a whole person with a diseased outer layer—as opposed to a diseased person.

I have a characteristic smell which is probably a combination of two weeks of accumulated ointment, sweat, and dead skin. A daily bath and change of clothing cuts it down somewhat but the smell does not quite go away. The pong pervades the entire flat.

23/9/01

Sartre was right about other people but he failed to mention furniture. Two men, one large table, and three chairs arrived in the flat at nine this morning. The men were movers and the furniture is my inheritance from grandma. The old biddy knew I hated that table. My flat is full. The table fills up the study looking blackish and huge.

Tina had three radios, a TV, and a PC in her flat, but had barely taken an interest in them for three weeks. The outside world starts with the epidermis, and it wasn't until her skin improved that she began to actually listen to the news instead of treating it as background noise. September 11 came gradually into focus as a major event, but the concept that the world around her had changed took longer.

Once, when looking out of her window, Tina saw Leon walking determinedly along the pavement. *I know him,* she thought. *He's local. He does things to furniture.*

26/9/01
I went to the hospital for a consultation. There was a lot of interest in my feet, and photos were taken. It was noticed that I had mosaic dermatitis on my thighs. More pictures were taken—fame at last.

The dermatologist seemed confident of my recovery. She said that things would improve from the top down. I suppose that means that I will keep my cracked feet for a while. An appointment was made to revisit in three months. A blood sample was taken. I topped-up with another bag of medicine.

Tina found a flyer from Nick Cob in her mail box. *Fencing makes a change from exhaust mufflers and pizzas. Buy now pay later.*

She also found a card with, 'How's the project getting on? Cynthia,' scribbled on it. Tina couldn't recall what the project or who Cynthia was. She put the flyer in the bin and took the card inside.

That night, Tina was creaming her feet with some noxious medication when the doorbell rang. She slipped a pair of plastic bags over her feet to save the carpet and shuffled in an old dressing gown to the door.

'Who rings at this hour?' asked Tina through the gap allowed by a chain.

'Opportunity knocks.'

'What?'

'I offer an opportunity for a beautiful lady to own the tallest fence in the street. It is Nick Cob at your service.'

Tina removed the chain and opened the door wide. *Why am I doing this?* Nick wore his track suit with a bow-tie, white silk scarf, and top hat.

'As you can see I am not beautiful,' she stated flatly.

'Buy my fence and it will make you beautiful.'

'I don't want a fence and would have no money to pay for it if I did.'

'The fence will give you money and beauty. Buy now and pay much later.'

Nick produced a scroll of parchment that Tina knew was a contract.

'This must be a dream. You are Mephistopheles and this is the story of Faust,' she said. 'Be gone with your contract. It's a bad deal.'

'It's a good contract. I worked all night on this contract.'

Tina—who had heard that Satan hated jokes about himself—replied, 'and you had the devil of a job getting here.'

Nick disappeared in a puff of smoke and Tina awoke in bed with plastic bags on her feet. She reached for the radio and found the card with its cryptic message, 'How's the project getting on? Cynthia.'

That was a ridiculous dream, Tina thought. *Satan coming to sell me a garden fence—I live in a flat.*

Tina had a moment of total recall. She was in a bar with a rather pushy woman about two months before. After a couple of gins, Tina had promised to write a booklet on the history of Lacuna. There was something else. There was going to be a fete celebrating the foundation of the suburb in December and—in the cab home—Tina had promised to develop some sort of theme for the fete.

'Too much,' she muttered, 'much too much. I need to get into the study, but first I must get rid of the table. I'll speak to that man about it if I can catch him when he's not walking.'

The Walkers

With the new identity imposed on him by the citizens of Lacuna, Leon found himself a hostage to whatever was broadcast by the media. One morning he got on the morning bus, bought his ticket, and confronted a row of angry stares from the fellow passengers. Instinctively Leon looked down at the change in his hand and saw that it was short. *I have to shop at supermarkets but I don't have to catch buses. If it's good enough for Martin Luther King, it's good enough for me.*

He got off at the next stop and started walking. Leon stopped at a café, and while waiting for his coffee, picked up a copy of the daily paper and saw on the front page the picture of a bombed bus and maimed victims in Tel Aviv.

On that particular morning Leon arrived at his workshop and found a notice of eviction from the real estate agent under the door. For years he had run a furniture repair and restoration business from the back of his cottage. At that time there were a dozen antique shops in Lacuna High Street plus many homes with older furniture requiring a jobbing repairer and French polisher. The business grew and so did the need for space. Leon found the smell of methylated spirits, beeswax, glue, and wood dust quite comforting but the neighbours didn't. In 1998 he went in search of a workshop and found one on a site due for redevelopment.

Leon was allowed to lease the place at a peppercorn rental until the demolition, due in six months. Three years passed and not a sign of a bulldozer. Leon took a pittance to the agent every month, but, apart from that, it was as though he and the workshop had been forgotten. Now he had one month's notice to vacate.

Leon had no reason for complaint, but he wasn't sure if the eviction was just to clear the site for redevelopment or because of his newly acquired notoriety.

There were now only three antique shops in the street and those economised by doing their own repairs. The current fashion in furniture was modernist-minimalist, but Leon was convinced that it was only a passing fad. The question was one of survival until the wheel turned. He was not going to pay market rental for a new workshop. *I'll work from home but I'll buy a few choice pieces and use the auctions. It will take a bit of leg work.*

When Leon had arrived in Australia as a youth, forty years before, he discovered one of the most diverse arrays of fine timbers in the world. It was still beyond his understanding that people could prefer radiata pine and particle board for furniture while grinding native trees into chips for export.

The Reverend Duncan Donald picked up the envelope, noticed the Canadian postage stamp, and knew it was his nemesis. He walked from the mail box to the manse like an automaton.

The Unreformed Presbyters had always been a minority religion. In seventeenth century Scotland they had been just a few dozen souls huddled together in a time of religious persecution. At odds with both the established teachings of John Knox and Anglicanism, by the early 1700s the flock only numbered a few thousand.

Then, with the great emigration of Scots to all corners of the globe, after the Battle of Culloden and the Highland Clearances, the Unreformed Presbyters had a renaissance. The insular creed struck a cord with lonely Scots in the lumber camps and mining towns of America and the British Empire. Little kirks sprouted up around the globe, but that was now all over. The Scots had been ideal immigrants, and their descendents became Canadians, Americans, Australians and New Zealanders. They had either abandoned religion or joined more dynamic faiths. The Lacuna kirk was the last in existence south of the equator and one of the few left outside of Canada and Scotland.

Administration of the Unreformed Presbyters had passed to Canada forty years previously. A board of trustees controlled the sale of property, as each kirk closed around the world, and dispensed the proceeds to worthy causes.

The Lacuna kirk had been treated with great toleration because of its status as the last outpost in the Antipodes. Duncan Donald had been subsidised with a stipend and free housing while he attended to his diminishing flock, but there was a limitation to the patience of head office.

On the days following the news of a mass breakout of refugees from an internment camp, police cars cruised slowly past Leon as he walked down the street. He didn't know if they suspected him of being a runaway or merely someone who could be hiding one. Leon would have sheltered an escapee if one had knocked on his door—he considered it the right of any political prisoner to attempt escape. No fugitive called, which was probably just as well.

The fact that Leon started walking in preference to catching buses opened up a new arena of suspicion. Lacunars were not great urban walkers. Some jogged, or rode bicycles, or even walked on exercising machines, and a few had been on treks to the Himalayas, but they did not as a rule stroll down streets.

Many of the byroads of Lacuna had evolved to adjust to this lack of pedestrianism. The pavements were narrow, sometimes too narrow for two people to pass each other without one stepping into the gutter. In a few Lacuna streets the pavements had changed their function entirely and become parking places for four wheel drives.

After several days of walking down streets, inhabited by only Leon and the occasional sparrow, a whole new tribe of people appeared and they at first seemed to be blind. Individuals, sometimes with eyes closed, would try and walk through him. Usually Leon would step aside but on one occasion he stayed put and the other person stepped into the traffic. Sometimes these people roved in packs, marching in pairs across the pavement to force Leon onto the road. Occasionally car drivers played chicken with him when he crossed the street at pedestrian crossings.

Duncan read in the letter that an official from Ottawa was coming in three months to inspect the state of the parish and, if necessary, to administer the closure and sale of the property. *Three months,* thought Duncan. *I have a little time.* Next day he stepped out into the streets in search of a flock, but with no idea as to how he was to achieve this end. Remembering the story of the loaves and the fishes, Duncan packed some sandwiches and a flask of coffee in case anyone he met was hungry.

The fencing contractor stood at the foot of Leon's bed. He wore his familiar tracksuit. Leon could just make him out through a whirling fog that filled the bedroom.

'What do you want?' asked Leon.

'I want a chat. I hear that you intend to be a terrorist.'

'It has crossed my mind, but you just want a terrorist in Lacuna to frighten people and make them order more fences.'

'Yes and no. I also like mayhem. You manage to alarm people by walking down the street. After your morning stroll I get phone calls by the dozen for fences and locks. But please don't go into the park; there is no money in that for me. Are you or are you not going to be a terrorist?'

'Yes and no,' replied Leon. 'I will increase my walking. I will vary the times and routes constantly. You will get your mayhem.'

Tina Finch started looking out for Leon in the street. She saw him being elbowed off the pavement and took a photo of the event with her mobile phone. *He's become a pariah,* Tina thought, *I wonder if he feels that he is one. I believe that people let themselves go if they become outcasts, but his clothes still appear clean. What is odd is that he is being treated as a new arrival even though he has been here for years. It is as though the population map of Lacuna has changed, and its history is being recreated.*

Tina reached for the notebook and then thought it better that the text was not sullied by post-September 11 thoughts. *I must get a new notebook. I must get into the study. I must get rid of the table.*

Tony Bugeja was born a Londoner to English/Maltese parents. He has been an Australian citizen since 1976. Tony gained an Arts degree at Flinders University and a PhD in Creative Writing at the University of Adelaide. He has published a dozen short stories and reviews, and his first novel, *Special Risks,* has been accepted for publication. 'Dark Man Walking' is an extract from his novel-in-progress.

Lauren Pope

Grande Pas de Deux

I only recognized myself
that evening at the ballet—

        Balanchine, Petronio, Forsyth

when your hand reached for mine
        and sprinted

across the contours of my palm.
        It was then that I lived:

pas de trois, arabesque, piqué, plié

through the dancers onstage,
and felt your confidence

        mount
into grace
achieved in touch

        on the floor
of my hand:

        thumb, knuckle, pad, wrist
                in Bach's Brandenberg Concertos

allegro moderato, adagio, allegro, menuetto
        trio, trio, trio.

Then the curtain   clinked
on the hard wood floor,

the lights came on,
your courage faded,

and I sat staring at my hand
unrecognizable as ever.

Winged Epitaph

Everything has the same basic needs,
and even though I cannot land on
a branch with undeniable grace—

wings push back,
feet forward,
tail feathers up
or land at all

I can imagine the impact—
wings fall forward,
enclosing the breast,

then rise up
like the landing
of a gymnast.

Born in Los Angeles, California, Lauren Pope recently finished an MsC in Creative Writing at The University of Edinburgh upon completion of her first manuscript that she hopes will be published in the near future. Her current hobby involves exploring models of The Hollow Earth Theory on canvas. She manages the oldest nightclub in Edinburgh.

Passports to the Past

Passports to the Past

Dominique Hecq

How strange it is, to be standing leaning against the current of time.
W. G. Sebald

Only the grass stands up to mark the dancing ring ...
Judith Wright

If the past is a foreign country, then we are all exiles shipwrecked in the present. Our fate is fraught with risks. We need only think of *The Tempest, Robinson Crusoe, Gulliver's Travels, Lord of the Flies, Wide Sargasso Sea, The Fortunes of Richard Mahony, The Transit of Venus, The Commandant,* and *A Fringe of Leaves*. Then turn our thoughts to *Remembering Babylon* and *The Secret Rive*r. Different spaces—temporal, geographical, political, and textual—different risks.

'The past is a foreign country' are the first words from *the Go-Between,* a British novel I read when I was sixteen, marooned in my father's house somewhere in the Belgian countryside. And the idea that we are all shipwrecked exiles is supported by the late Edward Said who saw exile as the twentieth century's quintessential experience. Over twenty years ago, Said published an essay titled 'Reflections on Exile' in which he states that we have become accustomed to thinking of the modern period as spiritually orphaned and alienated, the age of anxiety and estrangement. Modern Western culture, he adds, is largely the work of exiles, émigrés, and refugees. At the same time, exile has become the 'fetish' of intellectuals.

A few years later and on a metonymic par with Said, Salman Rushdie wrote in his introduction to Günter Grass' *On Writing and Politics* that migration uses 'one of the richest metaphors of our age':

> The very word metaphor, with its roots in Greek words for *bearing across* describes a sort of migration, the migration of ideas into images. Migrants—borne-across humans—are metaphorical beings in their very essence; and migration, seen as metaphor, is everywhere around us. We all cross frontiers; in that sense, we are all migrant peoples.

Thus, it would seem that at the end of the twentieth century the predicament of Australians had become global. It is indeed the historian R.M. Crawford who, in the opening pages of his *Australia*, noted that 'the history of Australia is a chapter in the history of migration.'

All migrants experience exile in one form or another. And the trauma of exile in its many forms lurks behind the scenes in all of Rushdie's novels, and it remains a central question in *The Satanic Verses,* the work which contributed to ostracize him forever from his culture of birth. Interestingly, though trained as a historian, Rushdie chose fiction to explore the upheavals of the contemporary world and the immediate past, utilising the resources and freedom of movement intrinsic to the tradition of the novel. In *Shame* Rushdie suggests 'it is the fate of migrants to be stripped of history.' But exile enriches a migrant's sense of history. This is because the metaphorical possibilities inherent in the concept of exile enable us to expand on those of migration, adding to it a sense of multiple dislocations.

Starting from the literal meaning of migration and exile, one can move on to the metaphorical because physical exile is often the starting point of other forms of exile—cultural, linguistic, psychological, ontological, existential, and metaphysical. Besides, exile also invites a rapprochement between displacement and writing.

In my early years of infatuation with the work of James Joyce, I used to think that the experience of exile was truer for writers than it was for anyone else. Perhaps that was because I thought writers were almost always either exiles or migrants; and, because of the distancing inherent in their practice and predicament, they often captured more accurately the essence of existence. Of course, that is a Romantic fallacy, yet there is a wealth of poems and novels supporting the theme of the artist as exile in the Western tradition. Not surprisingly, it is that Romantic fallacy which underpins the colonial imaginary, from the inception of Australian literature right through to its modern(ist) manifestations. The need, indeed, the compulsion to think of 'here' in terms of 'there' seems to be an inevitable part of colonisation, with words in the gap between perception and memory as the passport to other shores, as it were, shores where the imagination is not necessarily precluded from taking off. The introduction to an anthology such as *Bards in the Wilderness* draws attention to the phenomenon as it affected colonial poets and explains it as a 'conflict between perception and memory, between what the poets saw and what they thought they saw, or wanted to see.' Perception implies an awareness of present realities, an awareness of the object under investigation; it is anchored in the here and now. Memory, on the other hand, implies a turning away from present realities to some other reality. There is the feeling that the present is somehow less authentic than the past, that the immediate experience lacks validity until it has been authenticated elsewhere, that is, checked against the past. This is the kind of vision that informs Barron Field's poetry:

> Next is a ship poetic, forasmuch
> As in this spireless city and profane,
> She is my home-wand'ring phantasy,
> With her tall anchor'd masts, a three-spir'd minster,
> Vane-crown'd; her bell our only half-hour chimes.
> Lastly, a ship is poetry to me,
> Since piously I trust, in no long space,
> Her wings will bear me from this prose-dull land.

Field's suggestion that Australia is a place without history is a commonplace articulation of the colonial imagination. The implication is that if the literary imagination functions at all in exile, it does so through images and associations that establish links with a reality which is located elsewhere. The impoverishment brought about by the experience of migration is quite aptly presented as *prosaic literalness*. It is as though the 'stripping of history' inherent in the process of migration occurs simultaneously with a stripping of metaphor.

For an expatriate writer to write out of a consciousness of homelessness is nothing new. Andrew Gurr tells us all about it in *Writers in Exile*, and it is certainly possible to account for explorations of the artistic imagination in terms of 'here' and 'there', with Europe being, in Shirley Hazzard's words, that 'other authoritative world' and Australia 'in perpetual, flagrant violation of reality'. This is an exilic and colonial vision: Home is in the 'old' imperial 'there'.

Conversely, Patrick White believed that true artistic imagination would see the possibilities of reconstitution in the fragmentation of an historical reality of exile in the here and now: new roots (he cursed), a new language (he cursed, too), and a new mythology drawing on the old. As if burnt by the colonial sun and branded by hubris, his artists and visionaries would gladly appropriate parts of the dreamtime in that country of the mind that critics saw as his aesthetic and spiritual home. This is an exilic vision, too. However, it is neo- or postcolonial, for White's novels textually inhabit a narrative space generated by European discourse.

It is nonetheless a vision that I found appealing for many years. If Joyce's *A Portrait of the Artist as a Young Man* made me restless, it was *A Fringe of Leaves* which determined my point of rest in exile. And I confess that when I started to think about this essay, I looked and looked in *Voss* and *Flaws in the Glass* for the phrase used in the opening of this essay, 'the past is a foreign country.' Such are the tricks of memory.

Suffice it to say, exile, writing, time, and politics have altered my vision. More recently, the 'history wars' have contributed to challenging what I used to think about the creative imagination. Reading Inga Clendinnen's feisty prose on the 'history wars', and the battle of fiction versus history in particular, gave me food for thought. Her essay entitled 'The History Question—Who Owns the Past?' prompted me to articulate why I am sometimes weary of historical novels. Unlike Clendinnen, it is not the rigorous accounting of facts that I seek in fiction. Therefore I am often annoyed by the utter literalness and patriotism of historical novels. And sometimes I am annoyed by their opportunism, which I don't think is merely envy. More importantly, perhaps, Clendinnen's insightful discussion of the history wars made me aware of the dangers of believing in a concept such as the 'autonomy of history', whereby the actual practise of history has developed over time in such a way as to declare its independence from every other form of knowledge.

This reminds me of what George Steiner says about the Holocaust in *Language and Silence*:

> I realize that historians are right when they say that barbarism and political savagery are endemic in human affairs, that no age has been innocent of disaster. I know that the colonial massacres of the nineteenth and twentieth centuries and the cynical destruction of natural and animal resources which accompany them (the extermination of fauna being perhaps the logical and symbolic epilogue to that of native populations) are realities of profound evil. But I think there is hypocrisy in the imagination that would claim universal immediacy that would seek impartial appropriation throughout the provocations of all history and all places.

You may wince at the 'universal immediacy', but Steiner had other means of nuancing his thoughts before postmodernism came upon us:

> To think of literature, of education, of language, as if nothing very important had happened to challenge our very concept of these activities seems to me unrealistic. To read Aeschylus or Shakespeare—let alone to teach them—as if the texts, as if the authority of the texts in our own lives, were immune from recent history, is subtle but corrosive illiteracy.

Steiner is obviously talking about those who should have understood the nature of the political bestiality at stake with regard to the Holocaust, but who rose to welcome it and give it ceremony and apologia in articles, books, and some of the media propaganda in Germany. Here lies the cultural importance of the history wars waged in books in Australia today: far from being conducive to cynicism or elitist despair, the intellectual ferocity with which these wars are waged in the media, seems to arouse the desire for change at the grassroots.

Writers in Australia as well as in other postcolonial countries have preceded historians in exploding the myths conveniently created as a solace to the disillusioned civilisation of Europe—note that *The Tempest, Robinson Crusoe, Gulliver's Travels,* and *Lord of the Flies* have their settings on islands. It is just that it took some time before writers saw themselves in those mirrors and before they saw that their world, like many others, had been full of cannibalism, colonialism, savagery, slavery, convictism and coolism, genocide and racism, religious bigotry and intellectual dishonesty, and moral hypocrisy and political treachery. Judith Wright stands out as a pioneer in that regard. In both her poetry and her prose (I'm thinking in particular of *The Cry for the Dead*), she was concerned with the reconstitution of Australia's Indigenous past, a past which she rightly saw as having been consistently either suppressed or romanticised. She mourned the near genocide of the Indigenous Australians, bemoaned the vacuum left in Australian nature and culture, spoke of her pain and guilt, and sometimes grumbled about white complacency. I believe that the history wars have jolted some of us out of our complacency.

Postcolonial societies like Australia face a double challenge: the challenge of re-thinking the organization and function of knowledge. This is because such societies face two kinds of corrosive power, two kinds of imperialism: the political and the capitalist. Thus, on the one hand, we are dealing with a political power structure that comprises, at least until recently, the division between the Indigenous and the white society—with more recent migrant groups occupying the place of radical Other with regard to the dominant group. On the other hand, there is the capitalist commodification of everyday life, including culture.

Once upon a time, one would have thought that a writer's apprehensions would have undergone radical transformations in radical times of historical reappraisal, revisionism and further dislocation, to capture the inherent experience of exile at the heart of migration and colonisation. It is indeed commonplace to say that there shines in the mirror of art nothing else than our consciousness—another Romantic fallacy. Perhaps now is the time to look again, equipped with the lessons of history and politics, including textual politics. We are here on fairly alien shores, though this is what Indigenous writer Kim Scott attempted in *Benang*, an imaginative blend of fact and fiction about the author's own experience of cultural dislocation. And in a way this is what Kate Grenville attempted in *The Secret River*. Unlike Kim Scott, Grenville was rapped on the knuckles for it. But of course, unlike Scott, she is not from a racially mixed heritage. So was she naïve? Was she imbued with the omnipotence or megalomania so often attributed to artists? It would seem that for a historian of Clendinnen's ilk this is the case. For Clendinnen, Grenville has not only misrepresented the cruel legacies of history, she has done so with the help of a dodgy methodology: 'Some engaged reading, some preliminary flexing of the imagination, a run, a vault, and presto! You are there.' Yet this is what novelists do. Novelists pursue narrative truth, and sometimes this is done at the expense of historical truth. But Grenville made the mistake of claiming the superiority of fiction over history in uncovering this truth. Moreover, to a certain extent, she has, as Mark McKenna suggests, 'depoliticised national history.'

In an attempt to transcend the cruel legacies of history, the Guyanese novelist Wilson Harris has time and again explored the past of his people through some intimate involvement with the possibilities of myth, a process he calls 'infinite rehearsal'. His vision is alluring. His book *The Infinite Rehearsal*, for instance, describes the creative process in his own fiction whereby the artist, convinced of the metaphysical impossibility of ever reaching the final truth, keeps approaching both the mystery of creation and the mystery of reality through constantly revised and re-visionary strategies, thus breaking the rigid mould of history into a capacity for another genesis, for regenerative hope. This is how Harris puts it:

> I know that in unravelling the illusory capture of creation I may still apprehend the obsessional ground of conquest, rehearse its proportions, excavate its consequences, within a play of shadow and light; a play that is infinite rehearsal, a play that approaches again and again a sensation of ultimate meaning residing within a deposit of ghosts relating to the

> conquistadorial body—as well as the victimized body—of new worlds and old worlds ... new stars and old constellations within the workshop of the gods.

A central theme of Harris' fiction is the exploration of the 'obsessional ground of conquest', a theme which Grenville, aware of the predicament of both settlers and Indigenous Australians, takes up in *The Secret River*. Moving from their adversarial context, from their opposite 'here' and 'there' worlds (though, like Scott, racially and culturally Harris has a foot in both), the two writers apparently meet on common ground even if in some respects, such as their use of language and allegory, they are very different. Yet even though Grenville's comments in various interviews (those about the truthfulness of fiction and the novelist's 'superior' insights into history which particularly infuriated Clendinnen) would appear to consolidate this aesthetic and ideological common ground, their respective cultural legacies estrange them in terms of 'agenda'. Moreover, it must be said that Grenville's book does not work in the post-Romantic modernist agenda that some of her comments are couched in. First, though one might understand her position in these politically correct times, by refusing to enter the consciousness of the dispossessed and focusing her narrative on the experiences and insights of William Thornhill, her main protagonist, Grenville perpetrates a mythology of Us versus Them, the basic model of colonialist discourse she is ostensibly challenging. Second, by dramatising the consequences of the encounter between colonisers and their victims, while exploring its possible interpretations through a self-reflexiveness shaped by feminist awareness and Foucauldian conviction (namely that language is power and that to control story-telling is to control history), it seems to me that Grenville tries hard to sit on the fence, or rather on the (ivory) ladder she erects above the racial *mêlée* in her text and in the context of the history wars.

There is a precedent.

Recalling the opening of David Malouf's *Remembering Babylon* with its striking image of Gemmy poised on the top rail of the fence where he hangs for a brief arrested moment, 'arms outflung as if preparing for flight', invokes an image that adumbrates the problematic representation of Australian culture as 'geminate' in the book, that is, part British, part Indigenous, and part subject, part object. Like Harris, Malouf sees himself as a recorder of culture in Australia whose vocation is to 'mythologise' the country's history and national experience in such a way that he might find, or forge, 'real spiritual links between us and the landscape, us and the cities, us and the lives we live *here*. In the current political climate, this 'us' raises alarm bells, of course. But this is not the point. The point is that *Remembering Babylon* appeared in Australia and overseas at the time of the Mabo debate in the international context of the Year of Indigenous Peoples. It was hard at the time not to see the book as an opportunistic bid for political correctness on the part of a writer who had never before registered in his work the existence of Indigenous experience and its place in Australian cultural identity. Germaine Greer did not miss the opportunity to voice her outrage. And Malouf's alleged opportunism also figured in the subtext of what came to be known as the Malouf Controversy. This is to say that imperialism creeps into fiction in many forms. In Malouf's case, its political and capitalist forms were noted by commentators. I suspect that despite Grenville's candid demeanour, opportunism also dictated some of the aesthetic choices she made in writing her novel. This could increasingly be seen as expected by authors confronted by the new market conditions. There is in Australia what Mark Davis has called a 'decline of the literary paradigm' and writers are carefully considering all market avenues for their books.

So in the end, what was the fuss about *The Secret River*, given that historians and novelists understand narrative in differing ways, and differently even amongst their respective peers? A battle over the turf we call the past and over who is best equipped to access it. A turf whose shores may be accessed, it would seem, on the condition of owning different narrative passports, for I am not sure that the issue is one of a bridling of emotion by intellect as Clendinnen would have it.

Why not have our passports colour-coded: green (blue-green) where narrative is a text that merely awaits transliteration, and red where narrative is foregoing all the possible stories in favour of the story that is pressing to be told.

In art there is no proof, unlike, albeit limited, in history. And it is because there is no proof in art that novelists and poets write. There is no proof, merely the laying of oneself upon the alien, of questioning the spirit in oneself, and of accepting intuition as the gateway to the clues that erupt in a text—a text of endless potential, fluidity, and movement—as it moves away, acts upon one's resistances, and converts itself into something other than it first appeared to be, all within the scope of the past, present, and future. The end may be gratuitous, but then art was never meant to be a viable commodity.

DOMINIQUE HECQ is the author of *The Book of Elsa* (a novel), *Magic, Mythfits* and *Noisy Blood* (short fiction), *The Gaze of Silence, Good Grief* and *Couchgrass* (poetry) as well as *One Eye Too Many* and *Cakes & Pains* (one act plays). Her most recent awards are The New England Review Prize for Poetry (2005) and The Martha Richardson Medal for Poetry (2006). She currently teaches writing at Swinburne University of Technology.

JUNE PERKINS

WALKING CHILDHOOD

Learn to walk in your own feet
and be in your own skin
and then unlearn how to be in the ideas of skin
and walk in another realm
and in others' feet
across many textures of being

JUNE PERKINS (aka gumbootspearlz) has had 60 works published. These include photographs, poems, poems in visual arts exhibitions and installations, biographies, and academic articles in Australia and the United States as well as online. She has performed by invitation at Festivals and in Art Galleries in Tasmania, New South Wales, Canberra, Kiribati and New Zealand. She holds a doctorate from the University of Sydney (2004) and is currently an avid blogger (www.pearlz.wordpress.com) as well as an administrator of some flickr groups.

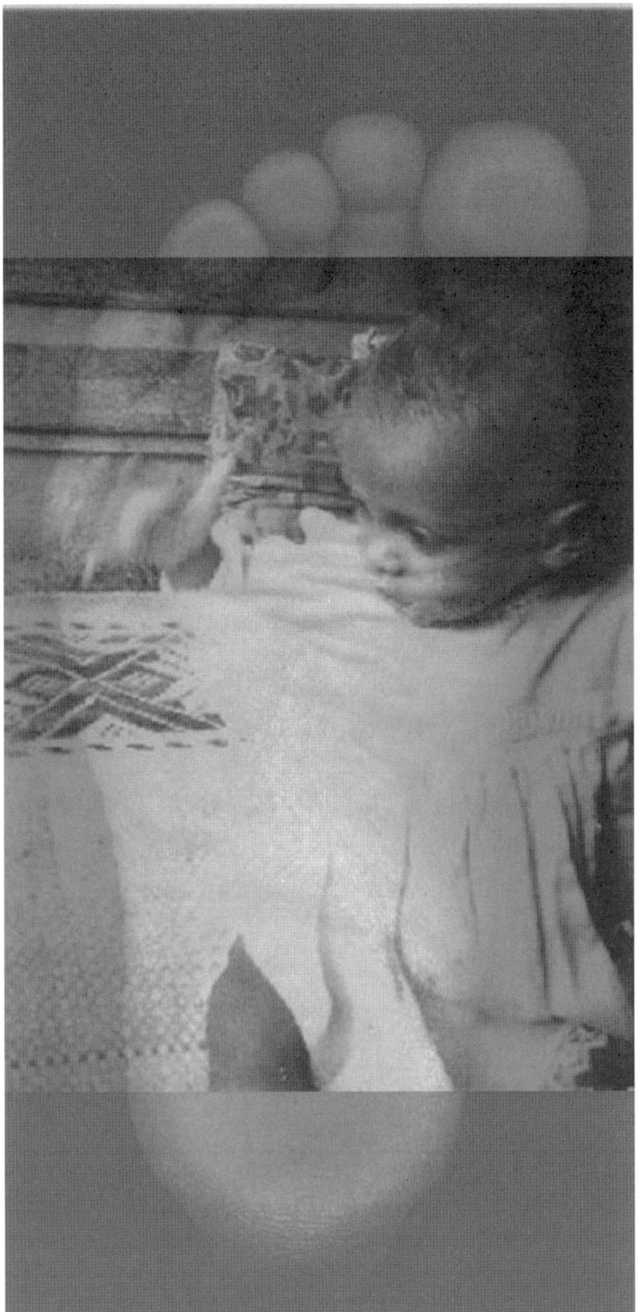

DRY

EMMETT STINSON

It was early evening in Adams Morgan when you decided to have your first drink in five months. A beer, cold and crisp. Everything that the humidity of Washington's Indian summer wasn't. Of course, it began as an impulse, a vague notion that a beer would be nice, but as you stumble down Columbia Road, looking down at the grimy sidewalk and then seeing all of the people going in and out of the CVS to buy condoms and Tylenol, it became a conviction. You needed a beer. There was no question.

But this is often how you do things—you feel something first as a sort of hazy, queasy sensation in your stomach. A yearning that's like hunger but isn't. Only much later will the logic of your desire work itself out. Until then, you are driven by your instincts, and you have no choice but to follow them.

This was like that. How just a half an hour ago, you decided you couldn't spend another minute alone in your basement apartment under that refurbished townhouse in Mount Pleasant. You couldn't bear another second of the sounds of your landlords' two kids running around the first floor, their footsteps echoing down through your ceiling. Neither did turning up the volume on the local news help. And really, you just put that on for some company, just something to listen to while you ate your dinner—overcooked pasta and sauce from a jar. You tried flipping channels, but each station just beamed out two more faceless newscasters and they all had that same eerie smile, like they were all in on some hilarious joke. But you didn't know what the joke was, or how any joke could make someone smile like that. Their smiles looked carved, wooden.

You looked around the living room, your eyes resting on your shelves of CDs and books, but you'd already listened to all that music. And, as for the books, you'd already read all the ones you wanted to and have given up on the rest.

But then there was the feeling in your stomach, and so you gave in—let your body take over. You got up, got out of the basement, and walked—even though you didn't know why or where, you did. Just grabbed the keys and left.

So now here you are walking down the street when you realize that you want a beer, and then you realize, hey, maybe that's what you wanted all along. What you'd wanted back at the house, why something inside you made you get up and get moving. It didn't make too much sense, of course, because there were bars much closer than where you'd walked, but, whatever, at least you've figured out what the whole process was about.

You look at all the people on the street coming and going. Not one of them but all of them—just going, moving. Like Pound's 'Station of the Metro.' This makes sense, too. All these people in movement with destinations irrelevant, secondary to the need for movement. Because Washington's like that, a transitional city. You can almost feel the city rotating on its own axis like a huge revolving door. A place people move to and then away from, with all the regularity of Congressional terms. That's how you ended up here, too—just a place to go after college, a place solidified into reality by the cool granite of its monuments. Most of your friends have moved on, too, back to graduate school or to New York or L.A., but you've stayed from love or inertia.

Turning onto Columbia, you feel the pull of the street sloping downward, and suddenly you know where you're going—the Pharmacy Bar. Why? Because it's dark and cool, and it's empty at this time of night and it's also the only decent bar on the entire street that also has a good jukebox. And that's something.

So you pass all the restaurants and the cheesy clubs and the only decent record store in town (it closed down six months ago) and then past the parking garage the new half-million dollar urban yuppie lofts are just behind. And then there it is on the left, the Pharmacy Bar, with its little slit of glass at the front like a half-closed eye. You open the door and feel briefly the chill of the air-conditioning, which is good compared to the swampy humidity outside that makes your entire body feel gross and clammy.

You realize pretty quickly that you're the only one in here, and when you walk up to the bar, you see the bartender, a tall, skinny guy with dyed blonde hair and an ugly goatee. You used to know all the bartenders in here, but this guy's new. You've never seen him before.

'What do you want?' He looks at you like you're a nuisance. Like he's asking you an existential question rather than for your order.

'Just a beer,' you say.

'What kind?' He asks. He thinks you're stupid.

'Anything cold,' you reply. 'It doesn't matter.'

So he pours you something and you go and sit at one of the tables in the corner and you think about putting something on the jukebox, something slow and sad, like Nina Simone's 'Black is the Color of My True Love's Hair,' but they won't have that or anything like it. Maybe some Johnny Cash at best, but that's not what you need right now.

Because what you're trying not to think about is the thing that's followed you the entire time you've been walking. The first thing you see when you go home and the last thing you saw before you left: the picture of the only woman that you ever loved, that you framed and hung by the door after she left. The Turkish girl who smoked too much dope and bounced in and out of psych wards while you covered up for her, telling friends she was on vacation with her parents—unreachable. The one who showed you there were limits to love, that you can't fix someone who doesn't want to be fixed. The one who cut herself on her inner thighs and tried to hide it from you—only making love in the dark, locking herself in the bathroom for showers and covering herself in layers of towels. Not letting you into the bedroom while she dressed. Yes, there's her picture, you can see it before you even though it's not there. The one someone took on your twenty-first birthday, years and years before, catching her in three quarter profile, her smile confident and smooth, her light brown skin a highlight, a compliment, to the pale hands connected to the anonymous sweatered arms surrounding her—yours, of course—but that doesn't matter, because the picture was about her, happy, smiling, the way you met her, the way you like to think about her. But that was years ago. Before you realized you couldn't save her. Before you realized you couldn't save anyone.

And soon, the bartender with the bad goatee is over at your table and he's reaching for the beer glass that you didn't even realize was empty.

'Finished?' he asks.

You nod yes, but he just keeps staring at you, looking at you like everyone else does. Just waiting for you to leave.

EMMETT STINSON is an American living in Melbourne. He holds an MA in Creative Writing from the University of Adelaide and is currently undertaking a PhD in Literary Studies at the University of Melbourne. He is the winner of the Melbourne Age Short Story Competition, the ArtsSA Creative Writing Award, a Lannan Poetry Fellowship (USA), the Wagner Medal for Fiction (USA), and has served as poet-in-residence for *Vibewire Magazine*. His work has appeared in *Meanjin*, *The Age*, *Pindeldyboz*, *The Konundrum Engine Literary Review*, *Sleepers Almanac*, among many others. He currently serves as Fiction Editor of *Wet Ink: The Magazine of New Writing*.

Patricia McCaw

Holiday Girls

Mr McGuffin and the papershop:
his eyes bright as morning,
above the headmaster moustache,
lets me weigh the sweets
and cut Warhorse tobacco
for men with hands like coal.
Miss McGuffin, his flat-chested sister,
eyes canny, strokes an upper lip,
light with feathers, and talks Scottish,
soft and incomprehensible.

It's summer and my schoolbag has
lost itself forever in our house as we work
five days, not just Saturdays anymore.
The Belfast Tele van screeches outside
and throws a load of 'pinks' for men
desperate for the racing news.
A woman lashes me with her tongue
for giving her thruppence short.

My sister, younger and prettier,
gets off an hour earlier on account of being twelve,
and Mr Cardy, a customer, whispers to her—
but I hear: ' If you like I'll take you home.'
I watch his old grey face, and think of his wife
the district nurse, in her bed, sick, alone.

I see his car outside the window,
blotting the lighthouse view,
its bonnet face blank, and dull.
'She's to stay with me,' I tell him
and his eyes look fishy.
My sister waits on the seawall,
kicking her heels, full of temper.

Later I see Mr Cardy's motorcar,
moved up to Giovanelli's Café.
He comes out with two ice-cream cones,
and sits in the car, eating them both,
slowly, before he goes home.

PATRICIA MCCAW has made at least two major moves in her life: from Ireland to Scotland, and from long-time social worker to writer. She writes short stories and poetry and is currently finishing a novel. She spent last year doing a Masters in Creative Writing at Edinburgh University, during which time she won a poetry competition. Currently she teaches creative writing to second-chance learners, enjoying the encouragement she can give to other late-starters.

BAR-BAR

ANTHONY KANE EVANS

1

It's what you get for taking an interest. And don't blame me for that title, it's not mine. When Neil hung himself I was upset for maybe a week but he was more an acquaintance than a friend, at least he had been those last few years. So the tear in the left eye, the clogged lungs, didn't last too long. And then I received word from his solicitor telling me that he had made me his literary executor.

'Literary executor? But he was unpublished,' I exclaimed down the phone.

'Nevertheless,' came the solemn reply.

Leaving the solicitors, I bumped into Anne, his ex-girlfriend. She was carrying a cactus.

'What did *you* get?' she asked.

'His complete and *un*expurgated *un*published writings. And you?'

She nodded at the plant. 'His entire cactus collection.'

'I'm not going to do it,' I said.

'Do what?'

'Reconstruct or edit or whatever it is that I'm supposed to do with all these papers. I mean, look at them.' I opened the thick briefcase and took out a sheaf of paper, waving the pages around. 'Look, just look: *Bar-Bar*, what is that supposed to mean?'

'*Bar-Bar*. I remember that one.'

'You do?'

'Yes, it's the one where—'

'*Stop*, don't tell me.'

I held my hand up, a little melodramatically I'll be the first to admit. But, I mean, what a responsibility to have thrust upon your shoulders. How dare Neil!

'I'll tell you what, Anne, I'll take a couple of cactuses off your hands if you sit down with me one afternoon and help me edit this ... this *Bar-Bar* story.'

One story, Neil, I thought, one story is all you are going to get out of me.

2

The café was quiet. It was eleven in the morning. Anne arrived late, putting two cactus plants down on the blue-painted table between us.

'Is it cactuses or cacti if there are more than one?' she asked.

'It depends what you're trying to get them to rhyme with,' I said.

There was a short pause.

'Mark, why did you ever give up writing poetry?'

'Because I was no good, that's why.'

'But you had that poem published in that Edinburgh magazine. I remember how green with envy Neil was.'

I snorted.

'Neil thought it was very good,' she said.

'Anne, forget Neil, he's dead. Did *you* like it?'

'I think I would have ... if I could have understood it. Do you want another coffee?'

'Yes please. I'm drinking the Kenyan.'

She went over to the counter and I took out Neil's story. I'd put it into a folder of its own.

3

Johnny Bar-Bar was (not the elephant) very moral really. At least he used to take a high moral tone about certain things. However, at the same time he used to write reviews for a Danish soft-core sex magazine. A sort of Danish equivalent of *Playboy* or *Mayfair*. They used to have some hard-core stuff in the back, you know the sort of thing, a woman going down on one man whilst she's being taken from behind by another.

4

Anne came back with my Kenyan. She had a pot of tea for herself.

'Well then, how's it going?' she asked.

'I've only just this minute started to look at it,' I said.

'Oh.'

'What does this mean, here in parentheses, *not the elephant*?'

'Well, I guess he just means that Johnny is not Babar the Elephant.'

'But why even mention such a thing?'

'I don't know but it is in brackets and look,' she pointed, 'it's also written with a different pen—the blue ink is darker there. Maybe he was having second thoughts about the Bar-Bar name.'

Like I was having second thoughts about my role of literary executor.

'The story is told from the viewpoint of a woman, you know,' Anne said.

'Are you sure? It seems pretty much third person to me.'

5

Johnny Bar-Bar, however, was not his real name. It used to annoy him when people asked if he had adopted it because of a certain elephant. As you probably know, *barbar* is the term the Romans gave to any non-Latin speaking person. They claimed that all those who didn't speak Latin merely made a grunting noise which sounded like *barbar.*

6

'I mean, isn't that typical Neil, that pedagogic tone, and for crying out loud who doesn't know that?'

'What are you doing?'

'Can't you see?'

I put a big red mark through the whole lot.

'Now the story won't make any sense,' Anne complained.

'We'll see about that.'

7

Personally I always preferred the Greek poets and dramatists to their Roman counterparts, with the exception of Catullus and Petronius.

8

'What are you doing? There won't be anything left of the story, it's not a novel you know.'

'With any luck it won't even be a short story by the time I've finished with it.'

9

In fact this brings me to how I met Johnny. It was in the Copenhagen public library. We both reached out and tried to take down a slim volume of Catullus, our hands met, then our eyes. The rest, as they say, is history. Though, in our case, the marriage lasted one short sour year.

10

Anne pouted.

'You weren't married, were you?' I asked.

'Yes but it wasn't sour. Not until the end, anyway.'

11

The marriage was my fault really. I'm an old-fashioned sort of guy—

12

'Hey, I thought you said the narrator was a woman?'

'Well, it should be, it's supposed to be me.'

Now I was getting confused. I ran my eyes back to the top of the page, followed it through, read on.

13

I'm an old fashioned sort of guy and, as you may know, men cannot get married to one another in England. I didn't fancy moving out to San Francisco and I knew that if I remained in London I'd probably end up living in sin with someone. I'm not against others doing it. It's just that I personally wouldn't feel comfortable about it.

I decided to head out to Copenhagen and try my luck. I won't pretend that things are perfect here. There are closet gays in high places and the gutter press is the same here as anywhere else: when they are not running off at the mouth about Bosnians taking over Halls of Residences then it's negative stories about gays. If I look out of my window down at the corner shop I can see a poster advertising one of those papers right now: *Lesbian Strippers: We want to be millionaires.*

14

Anne had gone very quiet.

'Are you alright?'

'You deliberately picked that story, didn't you?' she said. 'He wasn't gay. You were always jealous of his creativity and now he's dead you want to hang him out for being a gay.'

'Anne, what are you talking about? It was you who suggested I should work on this very story. You gave me to understand that you knew it. And of course I wasn't jealous, I never wrote prose, only poetry ...'

She continued to sulk.

15

I guess I'm rambling. When I say I'm old-fashioned I don't mean that I'm Christian. I'm quite content to believe that God died up in the Swiss Alps sometime back in the 1880s amongst an avalanche of Nietzschean prose.

16

'You can't cross out Nietzsche!'

17

When I first met Johnny over that slim, elegant volume of Catullus' poetry I'd thought he was a poet too. I insisted he take the book. He thought I was being a gentleman whereas I'd just realized that it was a Danish translation and I wouldn't understand a thing anyway. But he wouldn't leave me alone until he'd bullied me into going with him for a coffee. He made no bones about his sexuality. He took me to a café called Pan.

At one point he took his glasses off. This was my *first* disappointment: his eyes were smaller than I'd originally thought. I didn't mind him being short-sighted or whatever it was that was wrong with his eyes. I didn't mind so much those thick glasses or the fact that he wouldn't wear contact lenses. But those small eyes looked a *teensy bit* beady. Later on I'd always insist he keep them on—the glasses, I mean. This was a bit awkward during lovemaking but I used to enjoy those—

18

I made to turn the page but Anne stopped my hand.

'I don't want to hear anything pornographic, not in a public place at least.' She kept her hand on mine. 'Look, why don't we go over to my place, I'll make us some lunch, we can finish it there,' she said.

'If it doesn't finish us.'

'Hey, you never read me that line about Jane Austen. You just crossed it out.'

'Neil always was a name-dropper. Who cares if he read Jane Austen or Nietzsche.'

'But they were his favourite authors.'

'And who gives a damn. The Catullus I can accept, the rest is going out and I think he would agree.'

I looked up. The light in the ceiling blinked.

'Did you see that?' I asked.

'What?'

'That light, it just blinked.'

'It did not blink, Mark!'

A brisk ten minute walk took us to her place. She had put some posters up on the walls. They were not in *terrible* taste but they were the sort of thing you see in every second café that doesn't have much of a personal style. One of the posters was Toulouse-Lautrec's *Ambassadeurs*. I took exception to that one but later recalled that it was probably because I had

had the same poster on my wall as a teenager. Did I really feel so bad about my teenage years?

'Do you like them?'

'I can live with them for lunch but it might help if you put a pot towel over the Toulouse-Lautrec.'

'It's typical of you to have an objection to a man of the people,' Anne said.

'*Toulouse-Lautrec*—' I began at the top of my voice.

'I mean Aristide Bruant, the singer in the poster,' Anne cut me off.

Whilst she beat some eggs for a Spanish-style omelette, she relayed Aristide Bruant's history. How he was born a bourgeois, but embraced the coarseness of popular conversation, the language of the streets and finally cabaret. How, when the bourgeoisie came into his club—Le Mirliton—he would address them as 'pigs' and worse. I must admit I was surprised and impressed by Anne's interest.

'If you want to,' she said, 'you can carry on while I'm cooking but *don't* leave anything out.'

19

But I used to enjoy those cold winter nights when they'd get all steamed up.

20

'When what would get all steamed up?'

'His glasses, you remember, he didn't like Johnny's beady eyes, he had to keep his glasses on in bed.'

'Oh, yeah.'

21

So, the smallness of his eyes was my first disappointment. I didn't mind the pointed little beard. It was all the rage: clean shaven except for a bit of bristle stuck on the end of your chin.

22

'Hey, those goatees were around in the mid-nineties, this story must be at least ten years old,' I exclaimed.

'So?'

'So how come you say you know it? And how come you thought the narrator was you?'

'He used to read me all his old stuff. I must have got it confused with a chapter from his novel ... *The Crab & the Octopus*, that was to be his *magnum opus*.'

'Not with this literary executor it won't be.'

23

I've never really been into poseurs. I mean, I like the decoration, the colour, those kinds of people provide. I feel it's kind of necessary. But that was the curious thing about Johnny, he was such a poor poseur in some ways and if you made a joke of it—like when I would call him only *half*-cool—then he'd become very offended. On top of that he had this crazy idea that he was a sort of Everyman. I found I had to stop my criticism of his more pretentious moments because whenever I made such comments I could guarantee that that very same evening we would end up in some discotheque like Woodstock where they played chart music and only 'authentic people' (read: working class) were allowed in. He loved the working class. I'm from them myself so I don't have that problem. Johnny was from the upper class though he preferred to fuck the lower but if you used a word like 'fuck' with Johnny he'd stop, no matter how excited he was, and explain that he wasn't fucking you but making love.

24

Anne cut herself.

'Are you alright?'

'Of course, I'm alright.'

'Here, let me do that. I'm an expert at cutting onions.'

I took the onion and ran it under the cold tap.

'What are you doing that for?'

I cut it in half and then ran it under the cold tap again.

'It stops you from crying.'

25

So, that was probably my *second* disappointment with Johnny. That he was a poseur but wouldn't really admit to it.

My *third* was when I discovered that he wasn't a poet. I guess I had wanted him to write me a love poem. An acquaintance of mine once told me that one of her lovers had written her a love poem and a year later she had ripped it up because she thought it was a bad poem. She has no idea how lucky she was.

Well, to be strictly honest, it wasn't so much his not being a poet that disturbed me as him writing for that sex magazine. I mean it was a heterosexual magazine, you know, and it wasn't hard-core, as I've already said, so you didn't even get any anal sex.

26

Anne burned herself.

'Shit!'

'Look, Anne, maybe I should take over.'

I sat her down at the table.

'You read, I'll cook, but when I say cross it out then you *cross it out*. I'm the literary executor, you got that.'

'Yes ... Mark, don't you think that last thing was a bit, well, a bit crude. I mean it was not like Neil at all.'

'The narrator is not Neil, is it? It's some gay guy shacked up in Copenhagen. I think it's quite funny. It's better than pontificating about Jane Austen, Nietzsche and Erica Jong.'

'Erica Jong?'

'*Gone*.'

'You said you wouldn't—'

'I can do what I bloody well want. If this story should ever see the light of day then I, as editor, will be held aesthetically responsible for its contents.'

We discussed the point further until I realized that Anne was just throwing words out into the air in order to avoid having to read the story herself. She was afraid what might pop out. Either she hadn't read it at all or she had completely excised it from her memory.

Evidently Neil didn't get down to sexual details very often in his writing. That novel he had been working on was all about a girlfriend who kept on asking his opinions about art because she did not have any opinions on the subject herself; later she became an art critic. When Pablo Llambias came out with his novella, *She Has a Balcony*, which contains the same story—even though it appears only as a single line, in parentheses, on page 9—Neil gave up work on the novel and began the slow process of drinking himself to death. Before pulling himself together momentarily and setting up the noose.

Did it never occur to him that Pablo might have got the story from somebody else? And even if it was an original Pablo story—and reading that novella it seemed more like a throwaway joke—then surely it was legitimate to take a line from somebody's work and use that as the basis for a novel. I mean, *Jesus*, Shakespeare spliced two of Plautus' plays together without batting an eyelid.

Anne busied herself with setting the table. She even opened a bottle of Chardonnay.

'To our working together,' she toasted.

I looked down at the yellowed leaves, at the faint traces of lead. Between pages ten and eleven there were a few photos from some Danish sex magazine. They showed pictures of a naked woman, Pia Nissen, blonde and distinctly not hard-core.

'You can carry on if you like,' Anne said.

But I preferred to talk about other things. Like how she had taken Neil's death.

'Neil wasn't Neil after that book came out.'

She meant Pablo's book. She had had two boyfriends since Neil. A sailor and a car mechanic.

'I didn't want another intellectual boyfriend,' she said.

'Well, I wouldn't exactly call Neil intellectual.'

'That is exactly the sort of thing Neil used to say about you.'

'And he'd be right.'

I don't know how we did it but we drank the whole of that bottle of Chardonnay with the omelette. Anne rooted around in the cupboard under the kitchen sink and came up with some vodka, which we drank with pure orange juice. My, it tasted good.

27

Not that Johnny reviewed *sex* films for the sex magazine. No, he reviewed the Hollywood product. It was straight reviewing. He was kind of fair to his real opinions about the quality of a film except if he really didn't like the film then he tended to fill the space out by a rather mechanical re-telling of the plot rather than going for the jugular.

One day, after coming across *The Celluloid Closet* on Johnny's bookshelf, I asked him why he didn't review films for a gay paper. There are a couple of fairly decent ones up here. But he just stared me down and that night we ended up in Woodstock.

How many does that make? Three. That's right. Three down, two to go.

28

'How many what?'

'Complaints or disappointments.'

'Oh.'

29

I mean, I'm not going to mention all the little things: never putting the top back on the toothpaste tube, never cleaning up after sex.

30

Anne spilt her vodka and juice. The meat of the orange flowed over the last five sheets.

'Anne, how is it that every time sex comes up, you cut yourself, burn yourself or spill your drink?'

'Because I'm shy, that's why. I don't know you well enough to discuss those kinds of things. Or rather I do know you well enough but it's like watching a sex scene on TV with my parents or something.'

'I remind you of your parents?'

'No, not like that—oh, I don't know.'

I skipped the next line, which was in brackets anyway: (*I always had to throw the condoms away and get the tissue paper).*

31

The *fourth* thing was this major project of his. There is an unsung Danish filmmaker by the name of Ib Melchior. He wrote the film scripts for such sci-fi classics as *Planet of the Vampires* (It. 1962. Mario Bava) and *Robinson Crusoe on Mars* (U.S. 1960. Byron Haskin) as well as directing a couple of pictures himself, including *The Time Travelers* (U.S. 1960). But Johnny wanted to write a book about a ridiculous monster movie Ib Melchior had a hand in writing the script for, a movie many think of as being the worst ever made, *Reptilicus*, directed by a man named Sidney Pink. I mean, okay, what gay writer wouldn't want to write a book about a director called Pink. But as far as I can make out Pink was not gay. And the motor driving Johnny seemed only to be that the film was so absolutely awful. And it is, I can vouch for that, I've had to sit through it several times. But why not concentrate on the man's good stuff? I mean, he's eighty years old now. But, perversely, Johnny wanted to write a book only about *Reptilicus.*

32

Anne had shaken slightly on the word 'perversely' but otherwise seemed to be holding out alright. The vodka was working nicely inside of me and I allowed myself to wink at her. She smiled back.

I looked down. I didn't have far to go, it looked like the final two sheets were notes. Maybe suggestions for the re-write; maybe I should have read them before I started *this particular* re-write. Well, I thought, we'll see what comes out of it, if it's worth anything, if it can be saved or if it should just be consigned to the dustbin. Literary executor, *Jesus!* If I get this thing published maybe I'll just put that little title on my gravestone.

Anne filled my glass.

'Hey, easy on the vodka, this is serious work, you know.'

We both laughed. The light bulb in the lamp behind Anne flickered.

'I don't care!' I shouted at it.

'You what?'

'Sorry, I just misread a line.'

33

The fifth and final thing is my poetry. I mean, I know it's in English but Johnny was very good at English—all the Danes are—and after living with me for a year he was still good at it. That's supposed to be kind of a joke. But, seriously, my life is my poetry.

I have written two collections to date, *Zebra-Striped & Laughing* and *Red-Rumped & Crying.* The first is a bit artificial but the second is, I believe, quite authentic. However, I need people to *read* my poetry—and I don't mean literary agents, they'll come later—so I said to myself, *okay, when Johnny's read the second collection I'll post it off to an agent and maybe send it out to a publisher or two*. I'm quite confident. My lyrics are rather robust: hard-boiled poetry, I call my style. And I don't avoid my sexuality either. I'm quite proud of it, actually, when it comes right down to it. I don't care if *Red-Rumped & Crying* doesn't get published. But I felt I would have been ready to send it out *after Johnny had read it.*

But I began to suspect that Johnny had as little respect for my work as I had for his. This was a rather sad conclusion. I would like to have been able to respect Johnny's work but I couldn't. If he had just said that he was writing the film reviews to make money then it would have been okay, you know. But he didn't. He claimed it was serious. He would take the poetry collection if I put it into his hands, then he'd read the first two poems, always the first two poems, then he'd put it down and go to the fridge for some beer. Then he'd talk about his day at work. About how hard it was. How he had had to sit through another Cruise picture. 'At least he's cute,' he'd laugh.

Have I left anything out? I don't think so. I meditated a long time over those five points, those five disappointments and then I kicked him out. Well, actually, *I* left; it was his place. He still calls occasionally, trying to meet up. But I've told him that I absolutely refuse to so much as to talk to him on the telephone when that little Swedish whore is around. I mean, *Rudy,* what kind of a name is that for a man!

34

'Is that it?'

'Yep.'

'What're those then?'

'Notes.'

'Read them.'

'*Can I link the Lars von Trier story with the Pia Nissen story?*'

'What Lars von Trier story?'

'I threw it out.'

'Oh.'

'Well, what do you think?'

She looked up at me.

'I think we work quite well together.'

I had to agree.

'Yes, but what about the story? Do you think we'll be able to find a publisher?'

'In a gay magazine, maybe.'

'Oh, come on, it has universal themes.'

'Like, what, *perverse sex*?'

'Like disappointment and jealousy.'

'I think we should try something else. I think he's written better stuff.'

'Like what?'

'His novel, for example.'

'His novel? It'd take us half a year to get through that. Have you any idea what a mess it is in.'

'I was with him when he wrote it, remember.'

'Yes, so you were.'

'Well, what do you say?'

'Are you serious?'

She smiled, leaned over and poured me another vodka and juice. I looked behind her at the two doors, wondering which one was the bedroom.

ANTHONY KANE EVANS has had around thirty short stories published in various magazines/anthologies, including *The London Magazine* (UK) and *Going Down Swinging* (Australia). Next up will be stories in *The Tusculum Review* (US) and *Bound Off* (US). He's British but has lived in Copenhagen for the last 15 years where he makes documentary films on a freelance basis for the Danish Broadcasting Corporation.

Gardy

John Cailes

'Take care,' he says, as though he means it.

You get all warm inside—until something reminds you that it's just a way of breaking off, and experience says you are vulnerable and to watch your back.

Look at Gardy. Engine driver. Forty-five years married. For the best part of forty-five years, each work-day morning as he set off for the plant, she said to him, 'Take care.'

'Be seein' yer,' he'd replied for the same forty-five years, and faithful as a sheepdog he'd come back each night. He'd peck her on the cheek and say, 'Good to see yer, Chickie.'

She'd giggle each time and say 'Mate'—just like that. It was a ritual, just like the seasons. Never missed.

Then, one day, out of the blue, she didn't say it—just said, 'Stuff it,' and walked out.

But he had caught the habit. Said 'Take care' to anyone. And each time he did, that knife cut a bit deeper into his—well, I suppose you'd say his soul. There wasn't any blood or anything. He'd just wince and his knees seemed to give a bit more.

Gardy was getting pretty close to the ground and he reckoned his next move would be his last and he thought he'd have just one more blow-out on fish and chips and he was standing in the fish shop there in front of the fridge when, he swore, a garfish laid out on a tray winked at him. His life changed in that second.

'Take care,' he yelled to the man behind the counter as he headed for the door.

'Hey. What about your fish?'

'Stuff it!' he said, as he sped through the veil of plastic ribbons strung across the fish shop doorway: 'I'm off.'

Sold the house. Pocketed the dosh. Bought a caravan, a fishing rod, line, tackle and a plastic bucket and headed south in the old Commodore.

Two years later, he was a permanent resident in the Park, knew everybody, and fish seemed to queue waiting for him every morning before they snapped onto his line; old shorts, sandals, jumper sometimes, T-shirt mostly and a rag hat the Salvos wouldn't look at.

'Take care,' Gardy'd say to each old girl in turn at other vans in the Park as he dropped off a share of his morning's catch and without fail they'd say, 'Why Gardy, this is a surprise,' and Gardy would say, 'You'll never be as surprised as I was.'

Gardy painted a big '45' on both sides of his caravan and he bought some of those personalized number plates for the old Commodore and you can guess what they said, and all day and later into the evening he'd sit outside if it was fine and talk to anyone who came along and say 'Take care' with a catch when they left.

Some people said 'Mate' with a nod of the head as they passed. 'Good ter see yer' Gardy would say back, most times without thinking much about it.

Most people's stories in books go along like this and then something big happens and they get happy or they die. Gardy's didn't. The painted '45's faded and he did them again. A few of the old girls in the Park left and some new ones took their places and a limb fell off the peppermint tree near his van and the toilet block got renovated. The old Commodore rusted out.

Gardy bought a bicycle—and a new plastic bucket, once. 'Take care,' Gardy said to the shop assistant. 'Mate', came the reply with a nod. 'Good ter see yer', Gardy said, as though he meant it.

It was Milly—'Frilly' Milly, the other permanents called her—whose 'Mate' with a nod just about knocked Gardy off his plastic chair. Straight off, Gardy changed his shirt, put on some clean shorts and took her six of his biggest garfish out of his freezer.

When the tourists on the site alongside Gardy's moved on, Frilly Milly moved her van next to Gardy's and fish went back and forth every day—raw new-caught from Gardy's, grilled to a crisp with chips and lemon from Milly's. Then Milly said, 'With me old legs being what they are, this climbing outa my van in ter yours ain't much fun. I might as well move in with yer, Mate.' 'Pleased ter see yer', said Gardy without thinking. And so Frilly Milly and Gardy became an 'item'. Wasn't long before the '45's disappeared and garfishes with extra long bills took their places—pairs of them, with tails entwined somehow.

But alone at his regular place on the jetty each morning, Gardy still remembered, and still imagined ... 'Take care', she'd say. 'Be seein' yer,' he'd reply with a nod. And as he picked up his bucket full of fish and his gear and began the long walk and bicycle ride back to the Park he'd be rehearsing in his mind the words, 'Good to see yer, Chickie' just as if she was as real as she had been for all those forty-five long years.

John Cailes was born in Western Australia. He has been a farmer, shopkeeper, bus driver, industrial supervisor, X-ray operator, school teacher and writer. Now retired, he is a gardener and studies Italian language and the theory of music. He is married with three children and one and a half grandchildren.

Your Letter

Jonathan Ball

Dear—

October 27

Thank you for your letter.

I received it in the mail yesterday. It was a pleasant surprise, to say the least. I hadn't expected to hear from you again whatsoever, let alone so soon.

Is it soon? It seems soon.

I knew it was from you once I saw my name. Isn't that funny? It was my name, not yours, that let me know who the letter was from. How you wrote my name. *James*, your *s* trailing, straining to leave. You always called me James—even my parents call me Jim, but you always called me James, because you knew it was what I preferred. Even though everybody calls me Jim and I don't complain.

It's sitting on my end table now. It smells like you. Your perfume, I mean. I hope that doesn't sound strange. I only say it because you mix your own perfume and so of course you smell unique. You do so many things yourself. I have always admired that.

Your handwriting is beautiful. I would have recognized it anyway, even if you had written *Jim*. Those long, thin letters. Reaching upwards, reaching out.

Thank you for your letter. Should I read it? I haven't read it.

It's not that I am afraid.

It's that I like this. Not knowing what it says, what gift you've given me.

What words. Those long, gossamer strands.

October 28

It will be my birthday soon. It must be a card. It feels so thick, so firm.

Not a letter at all then.

But maybe. Inside.

That smell.

October 29

Thinking tonight. Remembering that party at your friend Gwen's house, where I first met your friends. I felt like a zoo animal, standing in the kitchen, on display and aware. Under inspection. I seemed to pass. After some initial discomfort, preliminary grilling from Gwen and your closer circle, I was let loose into the wilds of the living room where the larger party was taking place, while they conferred with one another and passed judgements. I found you by the punch bowl, looking sad, and asked what was wrong. You said you didn't know many of the people there, which I thought strange. But then I realized that most of your friends were still in the kitchen, talking about me.

I didn't like you being so ill-at-ease, so I taught you a game I play to make myself comfortable when I don't know anybody at a party. You pick out and imagine what people are like on the basis of the shirts they wear. Then you match people romantically based on these assumed interests. After that the game becomes matchmaker, where you consider it your duty to bring these couples together, and to this end start talking to one while looking for opportunities to bring the other into the conversation. Then you always know where you are trying to go with the conversation and it becomes less of a struggle to talk to somebody new.

You found this funny but impractical. We began playing together and while we were doing this your friends poured out of the kitchen and into the party, led by Gwen, who made a beeline for us and told you that I seemed like quite a catch. Which was a comment meant for me, to let me know that I had been deemed suitable, at least until further notice.

After that the night was nice but not memorable—in the way that parties, although fun, often blend together when you think back on them unless something particular sticks in your mind. And then it is only those particulars that you remember. I remember you standing beside that punch bowl. After my examination in the kitchen, it was a relief to see you again. But you looked so alone. You were wearing your grey dress, the one that would look drab on anybody else but looks elegant on you. You had your hair down, straightened for the occasion. The only other times I remember you straightening your hair were the day I took you to my sister's wedding and the night of our first date, when you looked so different with your straight hair that I thought for a moment I had the wrong apartment. At the party you wore your hair down so that it hung just over your eyes, almost covering them. Your beautiful eyes. You held your glass of punch before you like it was something that could protect you and you held your right elbow in your left hand as if it was cold. I felt so terrible for leaving you alone. But then you saw me and you smiled and gave me a timid wave and I was struck by how different you look when you smile, and it made me wish you smiled more often.

October 30

I want to tell you something. It doesn't matter what your letter says. Things won't change. I will still love you and it will still mean nothing.

I don't mean to sound accusatory, or make you uncomfortable. I'm just trying to be honest. I know that I haven't always been honest. And I've always appreciated your honesty in the past. In the long run. Maybe not all the time, not *at* the time, but later, upon reflection.

So it doesn't matter. Whatever you've written. I will appreciate the gesture. I am happy to still be in your thoughts. I think about you a lot. It's not that I want you back. Well, of course I want that, but that's not what I mean. I'm glad that we didn't keep on the way we were. I don't want *that* back. I'd like to recapture what we had before. But it's not possible, I know that, so my thinking about it is really just a vague regret. I wish things had worked out, or at least worked out better. It's sad to be surprised by your letter.

Letters. I am always writing letters. Letters I never send. Letters I send and regret. Letters to myself. The occasional love letter.

You wrote me three letters the entire time we were going out. Three letters for the hundreds I wrote you. Four, I suppose, now. I kept them all. I still have them, in my closet, on the overhead shelf.

Do you still have any of the letters I sent you? I wrote so many. I would be surprised if you kept them.

I love your letters. I loved them, I mean. Well, I still love them, but I don't read them anymore. I just keep them on the shelf. I don't even think about them anymore, not really. It was only receiving your letter that made me think about those three old ones. But I still love them even though I don't read them or think about them anymore. You know what I mean.

I'm sorry for getting so upset. You couldn't help things. They change. And I was so difficult. Depressed all the time. It was a bad time in my life, and yours too. We were both so unhappy. Forced to *settle*. I wanted to be a novelist—I *still* want to be a novelist—but was stuck writing copy for the neighbourhood section of the paper, fluff articles that weren't even distributed in some parts of the city. You wanted to join an orchestra but were barely able to practice between your two waitressing jobs. I told you to bring your violin to my place, that you shouldn't have to lose your practice time just because of me, that I would love to hear you play. Or maybe we didn't have to see each other so often, maybe you needed more time for yourself, for your work. You asked why I didn't want to see you. That's not what I meant, I said, I was just trying to be supportive. You didn't say anything but I knew that you thought I was back-pedalling, that really I wished you would come over less often. Which was not what I meant, not at all.

We had so many arguments like that. Sometimes I didn't even know what our arguments were about. Something I said taken the wrong way or something I said to pick a fight when I was frustrated at other things in my life. Or something you said to pick a fight, but then you would never tell me what the fight was about, why you were angry. You always insisted that you weren't angry, even when you refused to speak to me except to pick a fight, as if you knew nothing but fighting. I remember our final fight, when you said you didn't love me anymore and I asked what had changed and you said nothing had changed and I said I didn't understand and you said that you didn't understand either and you looked like you were going to cry but you never cried.

I was so angry.

I hope I didn't hurt your feelings. I must have. I know I tried. Anyway, I want you to know that I don't hold anything against you. I guess I should've told you this before.

I can't believe that you wrote to me first. You, who never wrote to me. Things are better now. I'm better now. The worst is over. I'm okay. I want you to know that I'm okay. I still care for you but I'm not taking your letter as a sign that you want to try again or anything. I'm just taking it for what it is, a letter. Nothing more.

Maybe that sounds a little silly, considering I haven't read it yet. But I know you and I know that it'll just be a nice, polite, normal letter that just says 'hi' and 'how's it going' and that you are writing just to say that you still care about me though not in the same way, and maybe we can be friends. I'd like to be friends. I know you aren't writing because you want more than that and I just mean to say that I'm not sitting around moping and wishing that we could be more than friends again.

I sound so awkward. I'm just trying to be polite. I don't mean to sound strange. It doesn't matter anyway. This is just one of those letters I'm writing for myself that I won't send. I do this all the time. You know me.

I guess I wouldn't blame you if you didn't keep them. How could I expect you to keep them? Even if you loved them. There were so many.

October 31

Everywhere, masks.

November 1

I'm feeling better today. It was a real shock to get your letter. I'll try to explain. When things ended I was a wreck. You know this. But what you don't know is that after we stopped talking, after I got over feeling sorry for myself, I did a lot of thinking and came to realize that you were right. If I was a bigger man I would've seen that at the time. Things were wonderful, and then they stopped being wonderful. There's no point in trying to pin blame or point fingers. I've thought about it a lot, and I can't think of any reason why things didn't work out. There was no reason. It was just the case.

I suppose I should tell you how things are now. With me. Well, work is the same in most ways but I have started to look at it in another way. I am still doing the same stories, but I have begun to look at these as more than disposable fluff pieces. I've come to feel that it is important, in a world that can be so isolating, to have a sense of community. It's important to read about yourself and people like you, to feel that the things that you do matter somehow, to someone, if only in small ways. I remember the first time I read a novel set in Winnipeg, one that wasn't set in Toronto or New York or somewhere else. I remember recognizing the landmarks and looking at my world differently after that, as something that had value and importance, at my city as not just a place to escape from but as a place where it was possible to live. I think that was the first time I wanted to be a writer, or, rather, the first time I felt I *could* be a writer, that being born outside of Toronto or New York didn't mean I was doomed to a life without meaning. So I've started looking at my job differently. I'm not saving lives but I'm making people feel a bit bigger in a world that makes them feel small.

I've also been doing a lot of work on my novel, working steadily, not stopping and starting and rewriting endlessly like you'd remember. I scrapped it and began again, as I have a habit of doing, but for the last time. I'm almost done now. Of late, I've been living a rather solitary existence, heading home straight after work and writing and rewriting and plotting and not doing much else other than reading and watching movies. I haven't spent the whole last year like this, of course, only the last few months because I'm so close to the end. I've worked for so long on this novel and it's coming together at last, though I'm having problems with the ending. Maybe you'd like to read it. You always said you wanted to read it, but not until it was finished. I remember how frustrated you got whenever I started over, how you complained that I would never finish. Well, I'm almost finished. The book is set in Winnipeg now. I even put a few inside jokes in the book, for Winnipeg readers. And a few for you. You always said you wanted to read it.

You don't have to read it.

So I've been reclusive but I've been getting a lot done, and feeling better about myself and my job and in general. It was a shock to get your letter because it reminded me of the person I used to be. I'd almost forgotten that person but I think I may have become that person again, looking at the envelope, for a little while. But today I feel like myself and I'm looking forward to reading your letter. I've decided to open it tomorrow and read it as a birthday treat for myself. Since it arrived so close to my birthday I assume you say 'Happy Birthday' in it at some point, so that seems like the best day to read it. Also, I'll need some cheering up, you know I don't like birthdays. They depress me. Every birthday I have to face where I am and where I thought I'd be at that age. Well, even John Milton has written poems about this problem. So maybe I make too much of things.

People will be calling all day tomorrow. I'll have to make sure the phone is plugged in. I unplug it when I'm writing. It always seems to ring when the words are flowing, and then it's like a switch has been thrown, and everything is set to off. Maybe you'll call. My number hasn't changed. If you still know my address maybe you still know my number.

~~*November 2*~~

~~Did you try to call~~

November 17

I still have not read your letter. I was planning to read it on the second, on my birthday. But, as predicted, I received a lot of phone calls. That was how I learned that you were dead.

I got all the usual calls wishing me a happy this and good luck with that. I got all the usual offers to come out and have a drink but I told them all that I just wanted to relax and read today, maybe I would do something next weekend. I did not tell them what I wanted to read. And I wrote some more of my novel and almost finished it, but I was having problems with the ending. I would say that I always have problems with endings but I have never had to deal with an ending before, so I do not know. In any case, I wrote and listened to some music and relaxed and planned to open your letter after dinner. I thought I would order some sushi to treat myself. And I thought about how I should get out more and decided that as soon as I had figured out this ending I would take some time off writing and do the rounds, visit my friends and go out to the bar and catch up with people. Maybe even give you a call. To thank you for your letter. I was thinking about calling you when the phone rang.

It was Gwen. She did not know that it was my birthday. She asked if I remembered her and I said of course I remembered her, she was your best friend. I said I was sorry for not recognizing her voice but it had been a long time since I last talked to her. A *long* time, now that I think about it. You know how it is. Of course you know. When people break apart, how all of their friends, all of the people they know, are torn apart as well.

Gwen said that she hated to tell me but that she thought somebody should tell me. She said she wasn't sure if I would have heard because we had been apart for a year now and had no friends in common. She said that nobody was sure when it happened exactly but of course I know when it happened because I have your letter and its postmark.

I did not tell her about your letter.

She said she thought somebody should tell me because she didn't see me at the funeral and she thought I would have come. I would have come. She said that she always liked me and wished things had worked out. Then she said that she didn't mean it like that and of course it wasn't my fault, it wasn't anybody's fault.

She said that you used pills. She said that it was painless, but I do not believe her. If there was no pain, there would have been no pills.

I did not know what to say so I thanked her for calling and told her I did not know what to say.

I am not angry. I want to thank you for your letter. You did not need to send me a letter and I am glad that you did.

I promise that I will read it sometime but I do not want to read it now. But I did go to my closet and search out your old letters and take them down. I read those letters and every time I finished one letter I held it while I read the next letter. I want to thank you for writing me those three letters. You didn't have to write me any letters and it means a lot to me that you spent the time writing me those letters when I know you don't like to write letters. You wrote them not because you wanted to but because you knew it would make me happy to get letters from you and that means a lot to me, more than I can say.

I wonder if you kept my letters. I used to write to you all the time. I have not written to you for so long.

Every day. I will write to you every day now.

Jonathan Ball is a writer and filmmaker. His writing has appeared nationally in Canada and sporadically in the US, the UK and Australia. He is a PhD student of English at the University of Calgary, where he is studying experimental literature, and is the Assistant Editor of the literary journal *dANDelion,* online at www.dandelionmagazine.ca. He writes a humour column, *Haiku Horoscopes*, which appears at www.haikuhoroscopes.com. Jonathan can be visited online at www.jonathanball.com.